"Reading each page filled with Scriptu
quotes from some of my faith heroes w;
spirit. Whether your walk with God has ~~~~ ~~~~ ~~ ~~~~ ~~~~~~~~~,
this truly engaging book has a place in your journey."
- TERRI SORRENSON, Worship Leader

"God has graced Luanne with this extraordinary gift of writing, and
her newest book, *Daring to Believe*, is just as powerful as all of her
teachings. In my opinion, it's difficult to even compare Luanne to
any other writer because she is so simply and brilliantly talented
beyond compare. Luanne shines beautifully through her writing
while radiating the love of Jesus. I am blessed to know her, and I feel
privileged to read her genuine words she always shares with absolute
certainty and authenticity."
- MARLA MCKENNA, Best Selling Author,
*Manifesting Your Dreams*

"Luanne Nelson has such a way in her writing that makes a spiritual
and personal connection. This book is a great read that applies to
our times so accurately."
- MARY MARGARETTI, Children's Ministry Volunteer

"I so enjoyed the down-to-earth discussion of the Holy Spirit in
*Daring to Believe*. It was easy to read, and very well thought through."
- G. ROGERS, Counselor, Stephen Ministry

"Daring to Believe is a book that reminds you to rely on Jesus and
the Holy Spirit in all aspects of your life. Luanne does this with lots
of Biblical evidence and practical steps for your everyday life."
- RENEE GILHART, Arts Ministry Lead

# Daring to Believe

*You Have Unopened Presents With
Your Name Written on Them*

## Luanne Nelson

**Foreword by R. L. Bowen, Th.D.**

## Daring to Believe

*You Have Unopened Presents With Your Name Written on Them*

Foreword: R. L. Bowen, Th.D.

Author: Luanne Nelson

Proofreader: Lyda Rose Haerle

Cover Design: Luanne Nelson & Michael Nicloy

Interior Layout: Michael Nicloy

ISBN: 978-1945907760

PUBLISHED BY NICO 11 PUBLISHING & DESIGN, LLC
MUKWONAGO, WISCONSIN

Be well read.

Quantity order requests may be emailed to:
mike@nico11publishing.com

Printed in The United States of America

*And we know that God causes all things to work together for good to those who love God, to those who are called according to His purpose.*

*Romans 8:28*

Dedicated to my Mother

If "Jesus Christ is the same yesterday, today and forever" (Hebrews 13:8), then why haven't there been any healings, miracles, and wondrous works like when He walked the earth? The Power of the HOLY SPIRIT filled His disciples in the Upper Room on Pentecost after Christ's ascension into Heaven, just as He foretold. Why did that Power end when the disciples died?

The Truth is this: The HOLY SPIRIT is just as Powerful, is just as Present, today as He has been since the beginning of time. The HOLY SPIRIT always was, and always will be, forever. Miracles, healings, supernatural events, and wondrous works continue to this day!

# Table of Contents

# Table of Contents

# Foreword

## A Word Rightly Spoken

In this writing Luanne has spoken the word that we need the power of God now more than ever. God has not diminished nor has His power. We His people must pursue the path of holiness and righteousness as vessels of God to be used in miraculous ways in these final days before Jesus returns for His bride, the church.

God's Word is power and without power what is called Christianity is just religion. The greatest miracle is a solid commitment to follow Jesus. When He then fills with His Holy Spirit, signs, wonders and miracles should be the mark of every disciple of His.

Luanne brings you back to the basic but powerful reality that God is who He says He is and that He can do what He says He can do. By surrender we are the bearers of that good news.

A must read that will rekindle the embers in the life of those who are not satisfied with the status quo who want more. Do you dare to believe?

R. L. Bowen, Th.D.
*Founder/President*
*Midwest Bible College, Milwaukee, Wisconsin*

1

# Introduction

F ussing and kicking until I eked out the very last drop of the day, I slipped into a deep sleep without even realizing it. Dead to the world, I dreamed in the vibrant colors of the Spirit.

Hours later, awakening refreshed, renewed, and ready for the new day, I broke the night's fast with oatmeal sprinkled with blueberries swimming in cream. I grew up out in the country; the breakfast nook in the kitchen of my childhood home overlooked a pasture of Guernsey cows. Still sleepy-headed, I daydreamed about the days when I drank the milk from those lazy beasts lumbering through tall green grasses still wet with morning dew.

~ ~ ~

Saying my morning prayers, I sincerely thanked God for getting me through another night. He knows me. He knows I am not ready to leave this earth – no, not yet, please. At this age, in my many-eth decade of life, I do not take anything for granted. There is still so much to do. Apparently, He agrees. I am grateful.

Some people say God chooses His biggest sinners to do His work. It's true, at least in my case.

Many years ago, I left that idyllic place of my youth completely unprepared for this world. My mom cried and told me she would never stop praying for me; my dad warned me it was rough out there. He joined with my mom in prayer, covering me with their protection as well as they could from afar. I was nineteen years old, transferring to an old university far away.

3

I knew I was smart, and I was filled with wanderlust slathered with the icing of indignation. I could not imagine what possibly could go wrong.

Until it did.

Still covered in the thin, transparent skin of a baby bird, off I hopped right into the mouth of a dragon.

God knows what He's doing even when we don't. I knew my parents' prayers were answered when I careened smack dab back into God's care after decades of seeing too much, doing too much, sinning too much. He brought me back to the Land of the Living to write about it all, to share with you what His grace looks like, and to tell you – yes – miracles really do happen.

They happen the same as when Jesus walked in this world, they never stopped happening, and they will continue to happen whether we stand still long enough to notice or not.

There will never be enough days to thank Him for his mercy. There will not be enough time to tell everyone what He does for us. There is not an earthly vessel big enough to measure His unfathomable, infinite love for us. After all, if the sky was made of parchment and the ocean was an inkwell, there would not be enough of either to write the thank you notes to Him for everything He does for us every day.

~ ~ ~

My teacher and dear friend, Pastor Verissa, included the imagery of the sky and the ocean in the prayer she prayed while laying her hands on my twisted back asking God to heal me. She told me she felt sorry for me "limping around looking like Quasimodo." Those were her exact words describing what I looked like to her in my broken condition.

4

And yes, with my faith the size of a mustard seed at that time, because I had convinced myself I had used up any smidgeon of grace I had left, the Holy Spirit nonetheless saw that speck of belief in my heart and healed me.

Injured when I lived in Alaska, my back had been visibly curved to one side. The X-ray indicated my spine not only was curved to the left, it also was rotated. The doctors told me there was nothing they could do, there was no surgery to correct the extensive damage. They offered pharmaceutical narcotic drugs to alleviate the pain. I declined. My back frequently spasmed, a scoliotic hump had formed on the upper left side, my right leg was shorter than my left leg.

When she was finished praying in His Name, she looked at me and told me to raise my arms above my head, I did. My back cracked and popped loudly up into the right side of my head. It continued to pop and crack for the rest of the day. Thank you, Jesus! My back is straight! The hump is gone! My legs are the same length! I am healed! Thank you, Lord Jesus! Thank you! Psalm 146:2 says, "I will praise the Lord as long as I live. I will sing praises to my God with my dying breath" (Krueger and Nelson, 2017b, p. 119).

These verses, in my heart, come to mind:

"Jesus said to him, 'If you can believe, all things *are* possible to him who believes'" (Mark 9:23). "'But as for me, I would seek God, And I would place my cause before God; Who does great and unsearchable things, Wonders without number'" (Job 5:8-9). "'And now, Lord, take note of their threats, and grant that Your bond-servants may speak Your word with all confidence, while You extend Your hand to heal, and signs and wonders take place through the name of Your holy servant Jesus.' And when they had prayed, the place where they had gathered together was shaken, and they were all filled with the Holy Spirit and began to speak the word of God with boldness" (Acts 4:29-31).

Now, I am going to go outside and enjoy this gorgeous end-of-the-summer day and ask Him to organize my thoughts so I can tell you this story without missing anything important.

This, I know for sure, and I can tell you right away, "And we know that God causes all things to work together for good to those who love God, to those who are called according to His purpose" (Romans 8:28).

# Chapter One

## Miracles Do Happen

*Jesus Christ is the same yesterday, today and forever.*

*(Hebrews 13:8)*

If "Jesus Christ is the same yesterday, today and forever," then why did the healings and miracles from the days of the apostles stop? Why were the disciples filled with the power of the Holy Spirit on Pentecost only to have that power end when they died? The Truth is – the miracles and healings have never stopped happening!

If you ask most people what they have to do to get to heaven, they'll most likely reply, "Be good." Jesus' stories contradict that answer. Philip Yancy tells us in his book *What's So Amazing About Grace*:

> All we must do is cry, "Help!" God welcomes home anyone who will have Him and, in fact, he's made the first move already. Most experts – doctors, lawyers, marriage counselors – set a high value on themselves and wait for clients to come to them. Not God ...

9

God became man, and that way He went in search of sinners. (Yancey, 1997, p. 55)

"Jesus said, 'The son of man did not come to destroy men's lives, but to save them' (Luke 9:56). He seeks to make men 'whole.' Sound of limb and mind, full of faith and power, strengthened in the inner man by the grace of God. This is something to believe in and to use for the glory of God and the deliverance of stricken humanity." (Roberts, 1947, pp. 104-105).

"And the power of the Lord was present to heal" (Luke 5:17).

When Jesus healed the people of their afflictions, He removed the dread of disease, and He restored the stricken to good health and well-being. He created a new life in them, complete with the strength and the willingness to work for the glory of God.

The Apostle Matthew writes, "They brought to Him many that were possessed with devils; and he cast out the spirits with His word, and healed all that were sick, that it might be fulfilled which was spoken by Isaiah the prophet saying, Himself took our infirmities, and bare our sicknesses" (Matthew 8:16-17; Isaiah 53:4).

Jesus redeemed and restored, performing healings and miracles to save a profoundly stricken humanity who had been deeply in need of His love, His mercy – His healing.

He is God, the Son of Man, in search of sinners, the Good Shepherd constantly searching for the sheep on the edge of the cliff, those who are broken and hurting, those who finally see Him and cry, "Help!"

And so, He does.

## Creative Miracles

After His death and resurrection, Jesus promised to send a Comforter and Helper to continue with His work in the alleviation of the suffering of mankind (John 14:16). Today, exactly as was the case on the day of Pentecost when He sent the Holy Spirit, all believers in Him are commissioned by God to heal. "And these signs will accompany those who believe: in my name they will cast out demons; they will speak in new tongues; they will pick up serpents with their hands; and if they drink any deadly poison, it will not hurt them; they will lay their hands on the sick, and they will recover" (Mark 16:17-18).

Becky Dvorak, in her book *Dare to Believe*, writes:

> God, in His great mercy, did not leave anyone out of the picture. He said that by faith all believers in Jesus Christ can lay hands on the sick and they will recover. All believers in Jesus who choose to activate their faith for healing can minister healing. (Dvorak, 2012, p. 66)

Dvorak continues:

> As you study the Scriptures concerning your authority over sickness and disease, your faith will become stronger, and you will be able to receive healing for yourself and release it to others as well. The Holy Spirit is moving mightily throughout the whole earth, teaching the body of Christ how to activate faith for divine healing and to use this powerful tool to win the lost for Jesus Christ. (Dvorak, 2012, p. 66)

"Creative miracles" happen instantaneously. Happening right away, right then and there, a lump goes away, a tumor disappears, a broken neck is reset perfectly with instant mobility, the blind suddenly see. God takes away the sickness and creates anew. "It's not there anymore!" "It's gone!" The brain dead are resurrected, and spines are straightened!

## Practical Healing

Practical healing or "healing miracles" take longer. They happen over time; the paralyzed get up out of their wheelchair and walk with the help of a cane or a walker, and over time, their gait is completely restored; a spine injury is healed while the neuropathy abates over time; a club foot is straightened slowly with the help of braces. It is time-limited and involves a recovery period. Dvorak reminds us to "encourage those in the Word when their healing is taking time to manifest" (Dvorak, 2012, p. 69). Jesus performed a healing miracle when he cured a blind man (Mark 8:22-26).

Whether it's instant or happens over a period of time, both types of healings are manifested only by the miraculous power and grace of God.

As believers, we have the go-ahead to evangelize to the world at large, spreading the Word of God to unbelievers and anointing the sick with oil so they, too, can be healed (Mark 6:7, 12-13). God is filled with compassion for all of His children, constantly seeking ways to ready their hearts to receive His power and love.

Dvorak explains:

> The healing power is not in the oil; it doesn't possess magical powers. In the natural realm, it's an act of

obedience to the Word of the Lord God and a point of contact for the receiver. In the spirit realm, it's a symbol of the Holy Spirit. The act of anointing is a symbolic act of releasing the power of the Holy Spirit for healing. (Dvorak, 2012, p. 71)

Regarding the fallen world we live in, evangelist and teacher, Al Houghton, says:

We have identified the importance of accepting God's pattern of turning evil into good as we trust the Creator to redeem adversity. In Psalms we found Jesus to be both King and Priest. Without the King, we enable evil through passivity. In Isaiah 44:4 we discovered the promise of God's blessing on physical and spiritual children for a season of growth in what really counts eternally! Jeremiah 44:4 brings us face-to-face with the commitment to love what God loves and voice His displeasure toward what He hates! Jesus asked me if He would be convicted for hate speech under US law. I found Jesus' own declaration of what He hates and there is high probability He would be convicted! Our nation has entered a new level of rebellion. (Houghton, 2020, Retrieved from: https://wordatwork.org/wp-content/uploads/2012/06/2012-07.pdf)

Jesus warned us about deceptive miracles in the last days. He said, "False messiahs and false prophets will rise and show great signs and wonders to deceive, if possible, even the elect" (Matthew 24:24). God cautions us that signs and wonders are not a sure sign of His actions since they can be performed by false messiahs and false prophets. However, God's "elect" will, through the inspiration of the Holy Spirit, be able to discern the difference between false and true miracles, even though some will be so convincing that even they will nearly be fooled.

The Apostle Paul gives us the same warning about the false messiahs and false prophets: "The coming of the lawless one is according to the working of Satan, with all power, signs, and lying wonders, and with all unrighteous deception among those who perish, because they did not receive the love of the truth" (2 Thessalonians 2:9-10).

## The Doubting Thomas Effect

There are a few believers who have decided that since Satan will appear to work miracles at the end of time, the safest plan is simply to reject all miracles. The enemy knew this would happen and finds great glee in it, of course. It is a falsity straight from the mouth of the "father of lies" (John 8:44).

Supernatural events and miracles are indications of the power that God gives to His people when we believe in Him. This is especially true at the end of time, when God's people will manifest the power of the Holy Spirit to an extent that has not been seen since the Day of Pentecost, the day the Holy Spirit filled the disciples with His powerful gifts.

The Apostle John, Jesus' best friend and His loving disciple, gives us some help and direction: "Beloved, do not believe every spirit, but test the spirits, whether they are of God; because many false prophets have gone out into the world" (1 John 4:1).

How do we do that? "To the law and to the testimony! If they do not speak according to this Word, it is because there is no light in them" (Isaiah 8:20). We must compare everything we see and hear with the Word of God.

Satan, the enemy, cannot perform true miracles. Satan does magic, performs illusions. He's a copycat, a master of counterfeits. He is the father of lies. His aim is to trick you into hell. Don't fall for it.

Smith Wigglesworth, in his book, *On Healing*, cautions:

> This morning, we will move on to the gifts of healing. However, you cannot expect to understand the gifts unless you have the Holy Spirit. All the Epistles are written to baptized people, not to the unregenerate. They are written to those who have grown to maturity and now manifest the characteristics of Christ the God. Do not jump into the Epistles before you have come in at the gate of the baptism in the Spirit. (Wigglesworth, 1999, p. 140)

Wigglesworth admits the person exercising the gifts of healing has to be a person of long-suffering, one who has words of comfort for the afflicted. Jesus Himself walked in the grace from long-suffering; He was filled with compassion. Indubitably, we cannot help the needy and the suffering until we've reached that holy place that comes as the result of suffering.

There is no room for doubt in His steadfast love for us, His free-flowing tender mercies He's reserved for us. There are those who can be witnesses to healings and miracles and still be a skeptic if their hearts are hardened to this world, if their souls have chosen to shut out His Holy Spirit. Pride refuses to acknowledge brokenness.

15

As Wigglesworth states,

> "Oh, we must wake up, stretch our faith, and believe
> God! Before God could bring me to this place, He
> had to break me a thousand times. I have wept, I
> have groaned, I have travailed night after night until
> God broke me. Until God has mowed you down,
> you will never have this long-suffering for others."
> (Wigglesworth, 1999, p. 143)

It's true. Having experienced total brokenness and begging Him for mercy, He's always answered my pleas in His time, for His Glory, and for my good (Romans 8:28). I've heard His voice audibly, "You don't have to do that anymore" (Nelson, 2019, p. 357).

My prayer is this: "Please Jesus, render me humble and worthy to be Your servant. There is no other place for me to be in this world." Seriously. He knows.

I know, without a speck of doubt, and I'll tell whoever will listen – He is with us. I have come to know firsthand, absolutely nothing is impossible with Him.

# Chapter Two

## Nothing Is Impossible With God

*And looking at them Jesus said to them,*
*"With people this is impossible, but with God all things are*
*possible."*
*(Matthew 19:26)*

Jesus walked among us, ate with us, taught us how to pray, touched us and healed us, restored us, saved us, died for us. "Greater love has no one than this, that one lay down his life for his friends" (John 15:13).

"Your kingdom come, your will be done, on earth as it is in heaven" (Matthew 6:10). Always. Forever. Our Creator does not change. Jesus does not change. The Holy Spirit does not change.

## He Loves Us So Much

God knows how treacherous it is for us living in this fallen world. Jesus reassured us before leaving the earth that we would do greater things than He did. Believe Him. Trust Him. "Very truly I tell you, whoever believes in me will do the works I have been doing, and they will do even greater things than these, because I am going to the Father. And I will do whatever you ask in my name, so that the Father may be glorified in the Son. You may ask me for anything in my name, and I will do it" (John 14:12-14).

Say "Yes." All we have to do is answer His call and say "yes." Say, "I will serve you gladly, Father God!" Already baptized in water – we are made new, born again as we are baptized in the Spirit. Imagine being born again in the Spirit – a fresh start, new eyes to see Him, new ears to hear Him, a new heart to love Him! When we become willing Temples of His Holy Spirit (1 Corinthians 3:16-17), we honor Him and rejoice in His love for us; He uses us for His glory! Say "yes" to His call.

## He's Made It So Simple for Us

We are made from dust and He turns us into His Temples of the Holy Spirit when we answer His call and say "Yes." "Then the Lord God formed the man of dust from the ground and breathed into his nostrils the breath of life, and the man became a living creature" (Genesis 2:7).

Is there a Spark of the Divine when life begins? We know, the breath of life comes from our Creator. "God, who made the world and everything in it, since He is Lord of heaven and earth, does not dwell in temples made with hands. Nor is He worshiped with men's hands, as though He needed anything, since He gives to all life, breath, and all things" (Acts 17:24-25).

"Then God said, 'Let Us make man in Our image, according to Our likeness; let them have dominion over the fish of the sea, over the birds of the air, and over the cattle, over all the earth and over every creeping thing that creeps on the earth.' God created man in His *own* image; in the image of God He created him; male and female He created them" (Genesis 1:26-27).

Today's secular world demands proof of everything that only science can deliver. Science has become the godhead of the modern age. Seemingly devoid of faith, hope, or love, this neoteric tree of knowledge takes on the look of a sterile laboratory filled with men and women wearing shiny badges as proof of their brainiac-ness. Science has become the Church of the Forbidden Fruit, with its Canon of Criterion. Complete with the serpent in its branches, just as in the Garden of Eden, it continues to strangle the virtue of obedience to this day. Knowledge has become The Holy Grail to attain in today's secular world.

Interestingly, in 2016, for the first time ever, scientists were able to capture images of a flash of light that sparks at the very moment a human sperm cell makes initial contact with the egg, fertilizing it. "The discovery of egg cells' massive intake and later release of zinc defines a new role for this element in biology," said Louis DiPaolo, chief of the Reproductive Sciences Branch at the Eunice Kennedy Shriver National Institute of Child Health and Human Development (NICHD), one of the NIH institutes supporting the study (NIH, 2011, Retrieved from: https://www.nih.gov/news-events/news-releases/zinc-sparks-fly-egg-within-minutes-fertilization).

Well, how ironic ... while searching for the formula to create life, they've discovered His Divine Spark, His Breath of Life, His Creation, the very moment when He manifests His gorgeous divinity!

Without a relationship with the Light of the World, "When Jesus spoke again to the people, he said, 'I am the light of the world. Whoever follows me will never walk in darkness, but will have the light of life'" (John 8:12), there can be no light. "The god of this age has blinded the minds of unbelievers, so that they cannot see the light of the gospel that displays the glory of Christ, who is the image of God" (2 Corinthians 4:4).

## Saying "Yes"

Once we've said "yes" to Him, we learn how to nurture His Spirit within us. We learn that when we cling to the material world, His Spirit dims in us. However, through prayer, studying His Word, and serving others through Him, that spark turns into a flame of love constantly reignited by gratitude.

Faith is the meeting ground between your limited self and your limitless God (Roberts, 1947, p. 30). "Say the word and my servant shall be healed" (Matthew 8:5-13).

Science is limited. God is not.

Simon the magician was so impressed by the miraculous powers of the apostles that he tried to pay them to teach him their magic tricks; he was chastised by Peter for trying to "obtain the gift of God with money" (Acts 8:18-20). There is not enough tuition money in the world to attend classes to learn how to walk and live in His Spirit. Faith cannot be purchased, nor can love, hope, or wisdom. These are precious gifts from our loving Creator, from Father God, when we come to Him with an open heart. With Him, nothing is impossible. Kathryn Kuhlman put it this way in her book, *The Greatest Power in the World:*

> Beloved, that was the secret of the ministry of Jesus. Therein was the power for the miracles that Jesus performed. It was the power of the Holy Spirit working

in and through Him. That is the reason Jesus spoke of the Holy Spirit. Jesus told those who were close to Him regarding the ministry of this wonderful One; and then, just before Jesus went away, He turned to them and His last words were the most important words that He could possibly speak to them. Why? He was going away, and He was leaving this great responsibility with them. What did He say just before His feet left the Mount of Olives? He turned to that little handful and said: "Ye shall receive power, after that the Holy Ghost is come upon you" (Acts 1:8).

Ye shall receive power – power to witness, power to do the very things that He had been doing, because this same wonderful Person, the Holy Spirit, will come. Jesus said that He would send Him unto us, and through Him we would have power to live a life of victory. It was never in Jesus' plan that anyone of His own, that any Christian, should have a life of defeat. Jesus lived an undefeated life when He walked the earth, and He said this secret power that had been His would be ours now.

The Holy Spirit is given to the believer for one purpose and only one – to witness and for service. He was not given for spiritual picnics or enjoyment. Jesus never used the power and the person of the Holy Spirit for His own pleasure, and neither are we to use the person and the power of the Holy Spirit for our own pleasure. The Holy Spirit was given to us to witness and for power for service, and we need to appropriate

that which is ours today as members of His Body.
(Kuhlman, 1997, pp. 34-35)

Praying Medic (his pen name) is a former atheist who has
worked as a medic for decades. He experienced a dramatic
encounter where God told him He would use him to heal the sick.
He started praying with his patients and with strangers, too, and
has seen thousands of them healed.

He says this in the Forward of his wonderful book, *Divine
Healing Made Simple*:

> There are two trends in the Kingdom of God that are
> converging in this book. It's been evident for several
> years that God is doing something special with the
> topic of healing the sick. And it's been clear that God
> is taking His Church out of the buildings and into the
> streets. The result is that God has been performing a
> great many miracles of healings in shopping malls, on
> sidewalks, in the workplace, and yes, even in the back
> of ambulances. How fortuitous that He has given us
> this book as a tool to equip the saints for the work of
> this ministry. (Praying Medic, 2013, p. 7)

The Medic says, "Jesus was the original street healer. He
traveled the streets of Israel on foot, staying wherever he found
lodging. During his travels, He told people the secrets of their
hearts, healed those who were sick and demon-possessed, raised
the dead and shared the mysteries of the kingdom of God. This
was His lifestyle, and it could be yours" (Praying Medic, 2013,
p. 127)

The Medic maps it out:

After modeling this lifestyle, Jesus chose twelve disciples and gave them their commission. He gave them power, authority and some guidelines (see Matthew 10:5-14). He told them to:

Visit the cities of Israel

Inquire who was worthy

Speak peace to the homes that received them

Preach on the kingdom of God

Deal with sickness and demonic oppression

Things went well on their first assignment. So well, that a short time later He sent out seventy disciples to do the same things, with few changes to the plan (See Luke 10:1-10).

This is the model Jesus established for His Church. How strange it is to look at the Church today and marvel that we've strayed so far from the only example He ever gave us. One of the saddest Truths about Christendom is the fact that in most cities there are more than a dozen churches, but not one person with the faith to heal cancer. (Praying Medic, 2013, pp. 127-128)

Praying Medic has a vlog on his YouTube channel: PrayingMedic; and can also be found at www.prayingmedic.com.

Truly, nothing is impossible with Him; He has given us power and authority here on earth. We cannot buy our way into His ways; we do not become His soldiers by osmosis while spending time with His troops; we certainly can't intellectualize His gifts. We cannot think our way into Miracles. When we make a decision to be His and surrender our lives to Him, He manifests Himself through us in the most miraculous and marvelous ways.

*Chapter Three*

## We Cannot Think Our Way Into God's Ways ...

*And Jesus answered them, "Have faith in God. Truly, I say to
you, whoever says to this mountain, 'Be taken up and thrown
into the sea,' and does not doubt in his heart, but believes that
what he says will come to pass, it will be done for him. Therefore
I tell you, whatever you ask in prayer, believe that you have
received it, and it will be yours.*

*(Mark 11:22-24)*

## Toss the Textbooks

Toss the textbooks when it comes to miracles. You can't "learn"
how to have faith any more than you can learn how to have hope or
learn how to love or cook a real omelet without eggs.

Enter the charlatans on the stage of life. There are plenty
of them. Every false gospel preached under the sun is full of
promises made, promises broken, fake miracles, and fleecing the
flock by wolves in sheep's clothing. Simon the Magician from the
Book of Acts comes to mind once again.

There is speculation Simon went to the southern region of the European continent and started his own religion where he charged money for everything. Can't you hear him saying, "Buy your loved one's way out of heaven's waiting room with a few indulgences. Pay for an in-house ritual, and she's sure to go to heaven today!" His religious followers unwittingly became nothing more than his pawns to contribute to his wealth. Disobedience to that church got you thrown on a torture rack during the Middle Ages; presumed heresy could get you burned on a stake.

Sooner or later, you have to ask yourself, "Where did all the donated money go that was earmarked for Mother Theresa in Calcutta, India?" Think about it. There should be a hospital there the size of the Taj Mahal staffed with the best docs the world has to offer. Nope. Nada. Not a cornerstone brick laid for the place. Up until her death, co-missionaries there reported how she re-used hypodermic needles after rinsing them off under cold water and continued to re-use rags to clean and dress patients.

## Simon the Sorcerer - and the Seven Thieves

As in the plot twist in the 1960 American film, *The Seven Thieves*, false religions often encompass a masterminded heist with the full cooperation of thieves in charge over their sleepy minions. Since earthly money is impossible to spend in heaven, the twist in the plot is that the real riches truly are found in the grace so freely given to us by Him.

Satan can do anything except create life, which is precisely why it does everything it can to destroy it.

"For just as the Father raises the dead and gives them life, even so the Son also gives life to whom He wishes" (John 5:21).

Can you even imagine the jealousy and hatred the enemy feels toward the Giver of All Life?

The devil can copy, pretend, and fake miracles. Since it cannot create life, the enemy does everything it can to destroy it. Drugs, alcohol, cigarettes, overeating to the point of morbid obesity – all from the enemy in its mission to mortify the flesh and ultimately deceive and kill.

Abortion and euthanasia – more murder from the devil. Gossip – the murder of someone's reputation, inflicting tremendous pain and sorrow on the recipient. No wonder God abhors gossip and slander.

> For since the creation of the world His invisible attributes, His eternal power and divine nature, have been clearly seen, being understood through what has been made, so that they are without excuse. For even though they knew God, they did not honor Him as God or give thanks, but they became futile in their speculations, and their foolish heart was darkened. Professing to be wise, they became fools, and exchanged the glory of the incorruptible God for an image in the form of corruptible man and of birds and four-footed animals and crawling creatures. Therefore, God gave them over in the lusts of their hearts to impurity, so that their bodies would be dishonored among them. For they exchanged the truth of God for a lie, and worshiped and served the creature rather than the Creator, who is blessed forever. (Romans 1:20-25)

God specifically tells us what is expected from those who love Him. You cannot think your way into holiness or fake His gospel; it's all written out for us:

> For this reason God gave them over to degrading passions; for their women exchanged the natural function for that which is unnatural, and in the same way also the men abandoned the natural function of the woman and burned in their desire toward one another, men with men committing indecent acts and receiving in their own persons the due penalty of their error. And just as they did not see fit to acknowledge God any longer, God gave them over to a depraved mind, to do those things which are not proper, being filled with all unrighteousness, wickedness, greed, evil; full of envy, murder, strife, deceit, malice; they are gossips, slanderers, haters of God, insolent, arrogant, boastful, inventors of evil, disobedient to parents, without understanding, untrustworthy, unloving, unmerciful; and although they know the ordinance of God, that those who practice such things are worthy of death, they not only do the same, but also give hearty approval to those who practice them. (Romans 1:26-32)

Conversely, The Holy Spirit is just as Powerful, just as Present, and very Patient in waiting for believers to say, "Yes!" Healings, miracles, raising the dead, continue to be daily occurrences amongst believers, the ones doing their best to obey His Word and keep His Commandments.

There is not one passage in The Bible that tells us that the gift of miracles has ceased; people report the occurrence of miracles today. Every day.

## Enter the Charlatans

The naysayers and the ultra-religious scoff. They've been brainwashed into thinking that only their special brand of churching holds the keys to the kingdom. They are convinced their religion is the only true religion, their clergy persons have special powers, and, most importantly, their way is the only way to heaven.

Many of them still wear the clerical robes straight from the Book of Exodus as they carry around their external temples from building to building.

Then, there's the false gospel gang, spreading the fake good news of "let me tell you anything you want to hear." None of these churches have any power. They are spirit-less.

Trent Horn, author of *Counterfeit Christs*, writes:

> It seems like everyone wants to have Jesus on "their side." Sometimes, people are willing to even ignore or re-write history in order to make that happen. For example, in 1813 Thomas Jefferson composed *The Life and Morals of Jesus of Nazareth* (later known as the *Jefferson Bible*) by using a razor to cut out sections of the New Testament that, in his view described the *real* Jesus. Jefferson was a deist who rejected the idea of God intervening in the world, so the miraculous parts of the New Testament ended up on a literal cutting room floor. What remained was the story of a

33

wise moral teacher who was tragically killed and then buried in a tomb (Horn, 2019, p. 8).

"Therefore, *The Life and Morals of Jesus of Nazareth* begins with an account of Jesus' birth without references to angels (at that time), genealogy, or prophecy. Miracles, references to the Trinity and the divinity of Jesus, and Jesus' resurrection are also absent from his collection" (Reece, *Harper's Magazine*, December 1, 2005).

"In January 2013, the American Humanist Association published an edition of the Jefferson Bible, distributing a free copy to every member of Congress and President Barack Obama. *A Jefferson Bible for the Twenty-First Century* adds some passages that were omitted by Jefferson, as well as examples of the 'best' and 'worst' from the Hebrew Bible, the Quran, the Bhagavad Gita, the Buddhist Sutras, and the Book of Mormon" (Shapiro, 2013, Retrieved from: https://www.christianpost.com/news/humanists-create-new-jefferson-bible-deliver-copies-to-obama-congress.html).

Dr. Rodney Howard-Browne tells us in one of his books, *The Touch of God*, "I don't do anything in my meetings other than allow the Holy Spirit to come and have free rein. What is so beautiful is that He comes and manifests Himself and touches the lives of individuals in a wonderful way." (Howard-Brown, 1992, p. 7)

Howard-Browne continues,

> "It's not our power; it's His. It's not our ability; it's His. He wants us to rely upon Him and trust Him to put us over. Jesus said, 'Freely ye have received,

freely give' (Matthew 10:8). He said, 'Behold, I give unto you power to tread on serpents and scorpions, and over all the power of the enemy' (Luke 10:19)." (Howard-Brown, 1992, p. 7)

We cannot think our way into this.

Instead, we surrender.

We come to know, it's all His.

We are His.

I am His.

There are always those who remain skeptic, and even those who are amazed. Next, let's visit the medical community and see what they have to say about miracles, healings, and His Holy Spirit.

# *Chapter Four*

## The Medical Community Chimes In ...

*And he said to her, "Daughter, your faith has made you well;
go in peace, and be healed of your disease."*

*(Mark 5:34)*

## There Is No Rational Explanation

"Surprised, amazed, a true conundrum," some doctors say when witnessing a true miracle! Puzzled, in their white coats, they'll often say, "I've heard of this happening, but I've never seen it before." Recently, a physician, her assistant, my husband, and I joyfully thanked and praised God together in a treatment room of an Urgent-Care Center after a dramatic miracle occurred involving my husband's scalp. The deep gash on the top of his head miraculously closed and disappeared, leaving him holding the wet, blood-soaked washcloth in his hand as the only proof of his healed wound.

The Great Physician, the Holiest of Holies, heals us. Hallelujah!

Doctors are busy people and often cannot be there right when you need them. But Jesus comes when you call Him. His diagnosis is always accurate. He can cleanse every wound and heal every sickness. He won't force His medicine on you; He waits for you to admit your needs first. And the amazing thing is the He already paid the bill for your care on Calvary's cross. (Author Unknown, 2019, Retrieved from: https://www.backtothebible.org/post/the-great-physician-1)

In yet another documented case in a different hospital, the docs exclaimed, "I see it, I can't explain it. He was next to death a few minutes ago."

He laid in bed, comatose, close to death. In his fourth decade of living, he seemed to be in good health just a few weeks earlier. Now, a tangle of wires attached to his chest scribbled the story of his impending fate. His breaths were few and shallow. The medics had done everything they possibly could do to save him following a heart attack and a series of strokes.

As he fought for what was left of his life, two nurses agreed to pray in the Spirit together with me over him, sending pleas and praises to God to find favor to heal this man through the power of the Holy Spirit. Since no one was allowed to enter his room except his immediate family and the hospital staff, the nurses agreed to anoint his body with holy oil. The oil I handed over to them was the fragrant mix found in the recipe from Exodus 30:22-25.

## He Looked Dead a Minute Ago

Guess what?

To the complete astonishment of the medical community, this man arose from his bed by the power of the Holy Spirit and lived for two more years. Miraculously, he was able to get his life in order and turned his life over to Christ. He was born again. He was saved. Thank you, Jesus!

Scientists work diligently trying to explain phenomena like this; yet, these miracles and healings cannot be categorized.

From experiments involving hooking wires to people's heads during "brain mapping," scientists have discovered there are changes to the brain while the subjects are in prayer. "'Praying involves the deeper parts of the brain: the medial prefrontal cortex and the posterior cingulate cortex – the mid-front and back portions,' says Dr. David Spiegel, adding that this can be seen through magnetic image resonance [*sic*] (MRI), which render detailed anatomical pictures. 'These parts of the brain are involved in self-reflection and self-soothing.'" (Spector, 2017, Retrieved from: https://www.nbcnews.com/better/health/your-brain-prayer-meditation-ncna812376)

Spiegel is the Associate Chair of Psychiatry & Behavioral Sciences and Medical Director of the Center for Integrative Medicine at Stanford University School of Medicine. He notes that while these reflective regions of the brain are activated, parts of the brain associated with taking action are inactivated. Spiegel says this finding could play a role in why prayer helps people struggling with addictive urges. (Spector, 2017, Data derived from: https://www.nbcnews.com/better/health/your-brain-prayer-meditation-ncna812376)

In a study conducted by NYU Langone Medical Center, members of Alcoholics Anonymous were placed in an MRI scanner and then shown images that were drinking-related in an effort to stimulate cravings. Without explanation, the cravings were reduced when the participants prayed together. The MRI data showed changes in parts of the prefrontal cortex, which is responsible for the control of emotion and "the semantic reappraisal of emotion," the study cited.

The study was led by Dr. Marc Galanter, M.D., who is a Research Professor at the Department of Psychiatry at NYU Grossman School of Medicine and serves as Director at the Division of Alcoholism and Drug Abuse. Fascinated with this subject, he conducted long-term research into the role of spirituality in long-term AA members spanning over ten years. He noticed that AA members underwent a transitional period where they went from craving alcohol to a new status where there was little to no craving.

The reduced cravings, according to Dr. Galanter's study, is the direct result of the amount of time that passed following a personal "spiritual awakening" by the person in the AA program, marking a transition to a different attitude toward drinking. He noted that previous studies by other researchers regarding the role of prayer on drinking behaviors had found that alcohol abusers who reported a spiritual awakening also drank less.

## Prayer Changes Everything

Research participants assigned to engage in prayer (totally unrelated to drinking) every day for four weeks, drank about half as much as those who were not engaged in prayer of any kind. (Williams, 2016, data gathered from: https://nyulangone.org/news/brain-images-reveal-first-physical-evidence-prayers-reduce-cravings-alcoholics-anonymous-members).

Dr. Galanter did not explore these spiritual awakenings because he can't. I have come to know first-hand that these spiritual awakenings are miracles. I have been a witness to several of them.

Bill Wilson, the co-founder of Alcoholics Anonymous, experienced a spiritual awakening as have countless other members of AA since it was founded in Akron, Ohio, in 1935. Bill W. said, "The greatest gift that can come to anybody is a spiritual awakening" (Anonymous, 2003, Preface).

I am not diminishing the importance of the role of physicians. I agree with Kathryn Kuhlman when she wrote,

> Education is wonderful and please do not say I am decrying education. What I am saying is this: The Bible is different from law, medicine or any other teaching in the whole world. The Holy Spirit is its inspiration. The Scriptures have been given by the Holy Spirit. They can only be revealed to the hearts and minds of men and women through the Holy Spirit, and this is something that you cannot go to school to obtain. You receive the Holy Spirit on your knees and His revelations must come straight from Him. (Kuhlman, 1997, p. 20)

Twenty-two years ago, I attended my first Alcoholics Anonymous meeting. Days earlier, I had experienced a personal spiritual awakening while hearing God's voice. Awakened in His Spirit, with no residual cravings whatsoever, I knew I was in His care.

Arriving at my first meeting, I knew my life was a mess. It was comforting to be around people who were in the same boat as me at the meeting, some of whom had been sober for a few decades. Their lives seemed to be going well. I figured if they could do it, then I could, too. I wanted to learn how to do whatever they did.

There were two men leading the meeting, one was a man named Jim and the other was named John. Jim was wearing a metal halo, blinking Christmas lights twined through the wires. I looked closer and noticed the halo was attached to his head by a few screws that had been drilled into his skull. I was mystified. Then, he told his story.

He and his wife were driving through heavy fog on their way home after a relaxing weekend in northern Wisconsin. His wife was driving, and she couldn't see the pile-up of cars ahead of them. In the thick of it, she slammed on the brakes and crashed into the rear of the car ahead of them. Later, they learned there were well over twenty cars in the jumble of twisted metal.

Jim's wife was a nurse; she looked over at him and saw him sitting up straight surveying the disaster in front of them. Since there was no blood, and he was sitting up straight, she quickly accessed he was not injured. She sprang from the car into action to help anyone else who may have been injured in the wreckage.

Jim continued to sit still looking straight ahead. He dared not move an inch. Moments before, he had felt a hand behind him gently lift his head up and tell him to keep still. He thought it was someone from another vehicle. He didn't know quite what to think, actually, because he knew his neck was broken and he was too afraid to speak. Everything had happened so fast. Moments before he had felt his head lifted, his chin was resting on his chest. Surely, he would have suffocated to death.

After sitting still for what seemed to be an eternity, his wife returned and realized something was dreadfully wrong with him. Next thing he knew, he was being put on a board and was slid into an ambulance. Then, he passed out.

The doctors were amazed. Looking at the x-rays, they realized his neck had been perfectly set. It had to have been perfectly set by the hand of God right there in the wreckage!

Surgery was not necessary to repair any damage – there was none – all they had to do was keep his skull set in place and let God finish healing it over the next few weeks. Hence, the halo.

That was the first miraculous healing I had ever really seen firsthand, although I would see many more in the rooms of AA over the next decades. He is with us. He knows what we need and when we need it.

Trust Him. Trust Him with everything. Trust Him with everything and learn how to truly take care of the precious life He's given you here on earth until we are called to be Home with Him. He sent His Holy Spirit to be with us, to heal us, to comfort us, to guide us.

Next, let's see what He says about taking care of ourselves on our way to holiness since, after all, we are called to be the Temples of His Holy Spirit (1 Cor 6:19-20).

# *Chapter Five*

## The Mind, Body, and Spirit Connection

*May God himself, the God of peace, sanctify you through and
through. May your whole spirit, soul and body be kept blameless
at the coming of our Lord Jesus Christ. The one who calls you is
faithful, and he will do it.*

*(1 Thessalonians 5:23,24)*

## His Pathway to Holiness

In the book, *Daughter of Destiny*, Kathryn Kuhlman's part in
miraculous healings is celebrated. The book is filled with firsthand accounts of true, remarkable, miraculous instances of God's
merciful healings. Here's part of one story:

> Perhaps the most thrilling stories were those told by
> the doctors themselves. Dr. Cecil Titus of St. Luke's
> Hospital in Cleveland said that a ten-year old's club
> foot "straightened before my eyes while Ms. Kuhlman
> prayed." Dr. Kitman Au of Burbank, California, a
> radiologist, told a newspaper reporter, "I have seen

healings in Kathryn Kuhlman's services that I, as a doctor, can only say go beyond human power." And Dr. Richard Owellen, the cancer research specialist from Johns Hopkins University, told of holding his infant child in his arms at a miracle service and watch the child's dislocated hip twist, under the power of the Holy Spirit, until it was healed and in place. (Buckingham, 1999, p. 198)

Testimonials often touch the hearts of those who do not believe in God. It's important to remember, "His mercy and grace – like the rain from heaven – falls on the just and the unjust, on sinners, as well as saints" (Buckingham, 1999, 197).

When Jesus walked this earth, He alleviated suffering, inspired nations of people to come to Him for comfort, forgiveness – and ultimately, gave us His perfect gift of redemption by sacrificing His own life for us. That wasn't the end of it. He promised to leave a Comforter, Helper, and Divine Healer for us to do the works He did while with us, and even more.

Jesus, God-made-man, walked in the Power of the Holy Spirit. This Spirit turned water into wine at a wedding feast at His Mother's request, healed people, and brought people back to life after they were dead. Jesus told us that we would be able to do greater things than He did when He was on earth through the Power of this Holy Spirit (John 14:12). All that is required of us is to have faith – and that faith can be the size of a mustard seed (Matthew 17:20).

One day, during his earthly ministry, Jesus met a group of people who were very ill. Suffering from the ravages of leprosy, they begged him to help them because they knew He could heal

46

them. That day, he did heal ten men from the scourges of leprosy. Of course, we know lepers were considered to be "unclean" and rejected by society in biblical times.

> As Jesus went to Jerusalem, He passed between Samaria and Galilee. As He entered a village, He met ten men who were lepers, who stood at a distance. They lifted up their voices, saying, "Jesus, Master, have pity on us!" (Luke 17:11-13)

Jesus, God-made-man, was able to heal them because he walked in the Power of the Holy Spirit. All ten lepers were healed, but only one returned to thank Jesus. Jesus said, "Were not ten cleansed? Where are the nine? Were there not any found to return and give glory to God except this foreigner?" (Luke 17:14-16)

Our mind, body, and Spirit connection demands more of us as we work our way into holiness because it is not for Jesus to wonder where we are ...

> I have to ask myself: Do I, as a follower of Jesus, truly thank Him for what He's done? Do I really understand and value the significance of what He has done and is continually doing for me in my life? Or am I one of the other nine lepers who went on their merry old way not giving a second thought to saying 'thank you' for the miraculous moments I've experienced daily? Do you? Do we just disappear after receiving what we ask God for until we need Him again in our next mess or crisis? I am as guilty as the next person for this: Bad manners. Rudeness. Often, we're rude to the person who loves us the most, whom we love the most.

The uncomfortable truth is we truly are more like the other nine who never said thank you than the one who returned to give thanks. (Nelson, 2019, *A Few Words on Your Identity in Christ*, p. 40)

Many years ago, on a trip to New Mexico, I sat at the airport watching people go by. I was alarmed at the number of people who clearly were obese, struggling with their luggage and carry-ons, out of breath as they sprinted to their gate. I decided right then and there to become a certified Health Coach. So, I did. Through a program partnered with the MacDonald Center for Obesity Prevention and Education (COPE) at Villanova University, I passed the exam and have been helping people get and stay in shape ever since.

My mission as a Health Coach is three-fold: to achieve and help others to achieve a healthy body, a sound mind, and a radiant Spirit. God gave us our physical bodies to "wear" during our lifetime on earth. When we invite God into our lives, when we become born anew into His Family, our bodies become the Temples, the vessels, of the Holy Spirit. It is our duty and obligation to take care of this precious gift within us. Our minds, filled with His glory, become dispensers of hope and love for His magnificent creation.

Kathryn Kuhlman reminds us of this:

The Holy Ghost's office is to regenerate, re-create, and quicken these mortal bodies, sometimes through works and miracles and healings. He also fills the "temple" of our bodies and will raise the dead at the time of the resurrections. Carefully consider these wonderful verses:

"And hope maketh not ashamed; because the love of God is shed abroad in our hearts by the Holy Ghost which is given unto us." Romans 5:5, and this one, "But if the Spirit of Him that raised up Jesus from the dead dwell in you, he that raised up Christ from the dead shall also quicken your mortal bodies by His Spirit that dwelleth in you" Romans 8:11. (Kuhlman, 1997, pp. 42-43)

## Pray and Obey

We are commanded to take care of ourselves. We house His Holy Spirit, and yes, God does know whether or not we choose to obey Him. It becomes obvious even to us as mere mortals.

> God doesn't ask much of us despite His generosity. He does ask us these very simple questions, though: Have we loved His other children? Do we love Him enough to remember to say "thanks" and do we love ourselves enough to even begin to realize His mercy? Do we love ourselves enough to take care of ourselves both physically and spiritually? Do we, really? (Nelson, 2019, p. 40)

If we disregard the gift of good health and well-being, we can expect illness in the face of disobedience. Alcoholism, STDs, gluttony, and a plethora of sicknesses are self-inflicted. Remember, since the enemy cannot create life, it does everything it can to damage it or extinguish it.

Smith Wigglesworth has this to say about sickness and good health:

There are times when you pray for the sick and you are apparently rough. But you are not dealing with a person. You are dealing with satanic forces that are binding the person. Your heart is full of love and compassion and all, but you are moved to a holy anger as you see the place the devil has taken in the body of the sick one, and you deal with his position with a real forcefulness. One day a pet dog followed a lady out of her house and ran all around her feet. She said to the dog, "My dear, I cannot have you with me today." The dog wagged his tail and made a big fuss. She said, "Go home, my dear." But the dog did not go. At last she shouted roughly, "Go Home," and off it went. Some people deal with the devil like that. The devil can stand all the comfort you like to give him. Cast him out! You are dealing not with the person, you are dealing with the devil. Demon power must be dislodged in the name of the Lord. You are always right when you dare to deal with sickness as with the devil. Much sickness is caused by some misconduct, there is something wrong, there is neglect somewhere, and satan has had a chance to get in. It is necessary to repent and confess where you have given a place to the devil, and then he can be dealt with. (Wigglesworth, 2006, p. 167)

We learn how to nourish our Bodies our Souls and our Spirits with the Truth to stay whole and fit on our journey toward holiness.

When we approach the Throne of the Most High with humility because we know we have disobeyed His guidelines for holy health (I see the Book of Leviticus as the Old Testament's Health

Manual), He hears us. In his loving mercy for us, if it is His will to be done, we can experience a Miracle.

In Kathryn Kuhlman's book, *Nothing Is Impossible with God*, A person who received a miraculous healing recalls and describes the miracle they experienced in the chapter called, "Healing Is Only the Beginning":

> "This warm feeling came over me as you left. I began to cry. Then I realized I could breathe normally. Look!" he said. "For the first time in eight years I don't have to take tiny little breaths." He was laughing and crying at the same time – but with normal breaths.
>
> Just then Miss Kuhlman called Don and me forward. Something had happened deep inside Don. Not just his lungs, but in his soul. I could tell it as he stood at the microphone, breathing deeply, joy written all over his face. Miss Kuhlman kept trying to ask him questions, but he could only say, "Look, I can breathe!"
>
> Realizing she wasn't going to get much information from either of us in our hysterical state, she put her hands on us and began to pray. I felt Don reach for my hand, and the next thing I knew, both of us were lying on the floor. I didn't hear anything. There was no definite sensation, just a marvelous warmth and peace settled over us. I vaguely remember hearing Miss Kuhlman say, "This is only the beginning. Your lives will be completely changed from this moment on."

Oh! How right she was! (Kuhlman, 2019, p. 136)

They went to the doctor the next day. The doctor was dumbfounded. They reported:

> When the Holy Spirit entered our lives, everything changed. ... We know Jesus is alive, not only because He healed our bodies but because He changed our outlook as well. Even though we're busier than ever before in our professions, we both feel we are missionaries, witnessing for the Lord Jesus Christ about the tremendous experience of being born again – and being filled with the Holy Spirit. (Kuhlman, 2019, p. 136)

## He Will Fill Us With His Power

Smith Wigglesworth says,

> We have come into a new order. We are dwelling in a place where Christ is the whole substance, and where man is but the body or the clay. The Body is the Temple of the Holy Spirit (1 Cor 6:19); within the temple, a living principle is laid down of rock, the Word of the Living God. It is formed in us, and it is a thousand times mightier than the "self" in thought, in language, in activity, and in movement. There is an anointing, a force, a power mightier than dynamite that is stronger than the mightiest gun that has ever been made. It is able to resist the greatest pressure that the devil can bring against it. Mighty power has no might against this almighty power, we speak about a substance of rock dynamite that diffuses through a person and

displays its might and brings everything else into insignificance. (Wigglesworth, 1999, p. 167)

Our bodies are what God gave us to wear while we live on His earth, we each are magnificently crafted by Him.

Truly, we must nourish our bodies, our minds and our Spirits with the Truth to stay holy, whole, and fit on our way to holiness, always remembering the mighty power of His Holy Spirit is alive within us.

To help us, God expressly gives us specific tasks to do, which we'll explore in the next chapter. When we follow His Holy directives, magnificent things occur!

# Chapter Six

## Do These Things

*He replied, "Because you have so little faith. Truly I tell you, if you have faith as small as a mustard seed, you can say to this mountain, 'Move from here to there,' and it will move. Nothing will be impossible for you."*

*(Matthew 17:20)*

## Have Faith the Size of a Mustard Seed

If people only realized the power our Lord God Almighty wants us to have, the power He is willing to give to us! He loves us all so very much. After all, we are His children, we are His creation. Smith Wigglesworth puts it this way in his book, *On the Holy Spirit*:

> Some people realize that they have had the power of the Lord upon them and yet have failed to receive the fullness of the Holy Spirit. Friend, what about you? God, in His love and kindness, has listed Samson in Hebrews 11 as an example for us. There came a time

when, because of Samson's sin, his eyes were put out. His hair had been cut off, and he had lost his strength. He tried to break free of his bonds, but the Philistines got him. However, his hair grew again. The Philistines wanted him to entertain for them, but he prayed a prayer, and God answered. Oh, that we might turn to God and pray this prayer as Samson did: "Oh Lord God, remember me, I pray! Strengthen me, I pray, just this once, O God" (Judges 16:28). God is "plenteous in mercy" (Ps. 86:5) and if you will turn to Him with true repentance, He will forgive you. Repentance means getting back to God. (Wigglesworth, 1999, p. 14)

The Power of the Holy Spirit is unfathomable and unmeasurable. Wigglesworth goes on to explain in great and loving detail:

What a wonderful and divine position God intends us all to have, to be filled with the Holy Spirit. It is something so remarkable, so divine; it is, as it were, a great open door into all the treasury of the Most High. As the Spirit comes like "rain upon mown grass" (Ps. 72:6), He turns the barrenness into greenness and freshness and life. Oh, Hallelujah! God wants you to know that there is a place you may come to, in which you are dispensed with and God comes to be your assurance and sustaining power spiritually – until your dryness is turned into springs, until your barrenness becomes floods, until your whole life becomes vitalized by heaven, until heaven sweeps through you and dwells within you and turns everything inside out, until you are so absolutely filled with divine possibilities that you begin to live as a new creation. The Spirit of the living God sweeps through all weaknesses. (Wigglesworth, 1999, p. 15)

The Holy Spirit changes everything.

Oral Roberts reminds us in his book, *If You Need Healing Do These Things*, that there are two requirements from God – faith and the willingness to go forth and sin no more (p. 19).

Serious prerequisites, don't you think so? Have faith and go and sin no more? What about all of those things being preached today? What about the "if-you-give-more-money-you-will-be-healed" according to the amount of your giving gang? Or the "you-do-not-have-enough-faith" group, you know, the holier-than-thou's? What about them? How 'bout the judge-y messes who preach the "you-must have-done something-really-bad" to be punished like that ... you know, the same gang of pals who told Job how God was smiting him for something or another. Many of the scutty spewers of such ridiculousness are convinced their religion is the only true religion, their clergy persons have special powers, and, most importantly, their way is the only way to heaven.

Well, they're all wrong.

Apparently, they've skipped over these passages in God's Word, "They will lay hands on the sick, and they will recover" (Mark 16:18), or this one, "Truly, truly, I say to you, he who believes in Me, the works that I do, he will do also; and greater works than these he will do; because I go to the Father. Whatever you ask in My name, that will I do, so that the Father may be glorified in the Son. If you ask Me anything in My name, I will do it" (John 14:12-14).

Ask the Holy Spirit to open your eyes and ears to the Truth, and you'll be set free to live a grace-filled life in the power and might of His Holy Spirit. Truly, these are marvelous days to be alive.

## Believe

Smith Wigglesworth tells this story in *On Prayer, Power and Miracles*:

> A man came to me in one of my meetings who had seen other people healed and wanted to be healed, too. He explained that his arm had been fixed in a certain position for many years and he could not move it. "Got any faith?" I asked. He said he had a lot of faith. After prayer, he was able to swing his arm round and round. But he was not satisfied and complained, "I feel a little trouble just there," pointing to a certain place. I said, "Do you know what the trouble is with you? Imperfect faith." "...what things so ever ye desire, when ye pray, believe that ye receive them, and ye shall have them." (Wigglesworth, 2006, p. 73)

God's complete plan for us is always this, "if you will believe, you shall see the glory of God" (John 11:40). I truly do believe God wants to bring all of us to a definite place of solid, unwavering faith and confidence in Him. So how do we get here?

R. T. Kendall does a wonderful job describing how the Holy Spirit uses the Laying on of Hands:

At some stage in the life of the early church there emerged a practice by which the power of the Holy Spirit was transferred through the laying on of hands. This was actually done some thirteen hundred years before Moses. "Take Joshua the son of Nun, a man in whom is the Spirit, and lay your hand on him" (Numbers 27:18). Moses did precisely that. "He laid his hands on him and commissioned him" (v.23) Note that Joshua already had the Spirit. But he needed more. There was both a renewal and a commissioning in the laying on of hands. Joshua was "filled with the spirit of wisdom because Moses had laid his hands on him" (Deut. 34:9).

A part of Jesus's ministry was that He laid hands on people or merely touched them for their benefit. He came to Peter's house and saw Peter's mother-in-law lying in bed with a fever. "He touched her hand and the fever left her" (Matthew 8:14-15). (Kendall, 2014, p. 174)

Have faith, have the willingness to go forth and sin no more (John 8:11). God knows we are all a pack of sinners; it's why He sent His only Son to redeem us and then sent His Holy Spirit to help us. When we get to know Him, truly know Him, when we have faith in His unwavering love for us, we become willing to go forth and sin no more. We become new, improved versions of our former selves. When we love someone, we go out of our way not to hurt them. Sin hurts God. It separates us from Him, and He misses us; Isaiah 59:2, Romans 3:23, and Hebrews 10:26-31 repeat the theme of how He misses us. It's why He sent us a

Helper, a Comforter – His Holy Spirit – to get us on track back home to Him.

## Have a Thankful Heart

Once we have faith and are willing to go forth and sin no more, we are transformed into new creations. Then what?

> For in six days the LORD made the heavens and the earth, the sea, and all that is in them, but he rested on the seventh day. Therefore, the LORD blessed the Sabbath day and made it holy. (Exodus 20:11)

God created the world and everything in it in six days. On the seventh day, even now, He continues to recreate us into the person He wants us to be when we make a decision to turn our will and our lives over to His care. What we often miss is this: Unless we are still, we will not even realize He's working on us. God does not need to rest, we do. What he's trying to say is "You need to be still on your day of rest, because I'm not finished with you, yet." And then, He goes to work on our Spirits.

Can you imagine if we were in charge of healing our own broken hearts and changing people's hearts around us? Only God, the Great Physician, can continue to heal what we cannot see and change what we are helpless to change. "But I will restore you to health and heal your wounds, declares the LORD" (Jeremiah 30:17).

He is the only One who can heal us and change us. God not only wants us to rest on the seventh day, He also uses the day to show us how to be a better version of ourselves. He wants us to be still to receive his blessings and corrections. He is continuing to create each one of us, shaping us into the persons he wants us to become.

God not only wants us to rest on the seventh day, He wants us to realize He's *blessed* this day and made it *holy*. We recall not just the physical Creation, but also remember the ongoing Spiritual Creation in each one of us. It's a holy time, set apart for God's use. Opening our hearts and spirits to receive Divine Holiness is not only about going to church and resting from work; rather, it's about opening ourselves to hearing His Word, prayerfully asking for forgiveness and cleansing – and putting the changes He puts into our hearts into action.

This Holy Day of the week is the day He looks past our human nature and breathes the holy fire of His Spirit into our new hearts when we avail ourselves to Him. This is the day He changes us – shapes us into what He wants us to be. This is the day we rest in Him to become refreshed, renewed, forgiven, healed, and changed. Even the gift of pain becomes a blessing, which we'll look at closer next.

*Father God, please make me new and improved.*
*Forgive me and give me a new spotless heart*
*filled with Your blessings.*

*Make me holy. Please.*

*Amen.*

# *Chapter Seven*

## The Gift of Pain

*In everything give thanks; for this is the will*
*of God in Christ Jesus for you.*

*(1 Thessalonians 5:18)*

I loved my fourth-grade teacher, Sister Naomi. One day, she taught us this Truth, one I've repeated many times over the years. She said, "God always answers our prayers." So far, so good. I was confident she was right about that since my Mom had said the same exact thing to me when I was really little.

She went on to say, "Sometimes the answer is 'Yes,' sometimes the answer is 'No,' and sometimes He says, 'Not yet.'" She wrapped up the lesson with this, "So, always know He's with you and taking care of everything you need in His own perfect way."

Do you see why I loved her so much? She basically covered all the bases so we would never lose faith in Him.

She didn't cover the subject of pain, though. We were too little. We would learn that lesson later in life. No one escapes it. No one gets through this life unscathed. Pain is just as much a part of being human as joy is, even though it rarely is discussed as one of God's gifts to us.

We usually are so well-fed and comfortable, that when pain does strike, we become loud whiners and kickers, thinking making that much noise will somehow alleviate our suffering.

The perfect pain in the neck even has a name and a face these days. Her name is "Karen." She's the quintessential do-gooder who messes up your hair and your life while she blithely pirouettes through her own perfect day. She doesn't really exist. Pain does, though.

## Pain Is Not Always Physical

In His love for us, God has limitless power to bring healing to our spiritual, mental, and physical health. The Apostle Peter summed up the ministry of Jesus by saying that He came to heal all who were oppressed by the devil. (Acts 10:38)

But how?

Oral Roberts tell us this in his book, *If You Need Healing, Do These Things*:

> There are a lot of things we would be better off *without*. Losing ourselves in obedience to God, linking ourselves with the limitless power of Christ, getting in tune with the Savior – these are the things that count most when we seek to be healed through faith in God. Lose yourself. (Matthew 16:25) (Roberts, 1947, pp. 91-92).

Roberts goes on to say, "The most thrilling question ever asked by the Son of God is, 'Wilt though be made whole?' His answer, then, was the same as it is now, 'Rise, thy faith doth make thee whole.' Faith does it." (Roberts, 1947, p. 80)

God honors our faith, our faith honors God.

Sister Naomi was right, sometimes the answer is, "Not yet." I think that's the hardest answer to accept, because I've come to know that in it, there usually is a lesson to be learned. One of the lessons I learned is described in *Tipping Tables: The Seven Deadly Sins and Stories of Redemption*:

> It has been twenty years since God relieved me of my alcoholism. In the few weeks following the Miracle, I prayed a lot and came to realize a few things: I came to know everything happens in His time, not mine, not ours. He knows the map of our hearts. Every single one of us. We are His children. He knows every hair on our heads. He knit us together under our Mother's hearts. I know He loves me – and you.
>
> ... I know now, He was not punishing me by delaying the Miracle for a later date, He knew I needed to learn to be humble. I needed to be prepared and ready to receive His generous Miracle. He wanted me to learn the difference between humility and humiliation.
>
> I came to know – and it still takes my breath away to this day – that when I am at my weakest, I know the magnificent force of His strength and the loving touch of His tender mercy. God's grace is sufficient to see us through, no matter what. (Nelson, 2019, p. 358)

God hadn't forgotten me, He wasn't ignoring me, He wasn't punishing me. He was refining me (1 Peter 1:7), He was redefining me. He was creating in me a better version of myself – for His Glory and my own good (Romans 8:28).

## The Solution Belongs to Him

Doesn't being healed mean we will be pain free? The answer is, "No."

> Blessed be the God and Father of our Lord Jesus Christ, the Father of mercies and God of all comfort, who comforts us in all our affliction, so that we may be able to comfort those who are in any affliction, with the comfort with which we ourselves are comforted by God. For as we share abundantly in Christ's sufferings, so through Christ we share abundantly in comfort too. If we are afflicted, it is for your comfort and salvation; and if we are comforted, it is for your comfort, which you experience when you patiently endure the same sufferings that we suffer. Our hope for you is unshaken, for we know that as you share in our sufferings, you will also share in our comfort. (2 Corinthians 1:3-7)

The word "comfort" is mentioned ten times in those five verses, two mentions per verse. Unless you've experienced affliction – and I think it's safe to say we all have – we cannot know the meaning of comfort. Comfort is only understood in light of pain, distress, or discomfort.

So, what about Paul's thorn, then? After falling and being

blinded, he arrived at God's door desperate and pleading for help. This was the guy, known as Saul, who was killing new Christians all over Rome with intense fervor and great zeal. Given a job, he was going to be excellent at it! Nope, there was nothing lukewarm about Paul. Later, when God saw fit to rescue Saul's pitiful self and rename him Paul, Paul's commitment would be trusted to pen most of the New Testament's letters on God's behalf. Paul unabashedly threw himself into the role of personal stenographer for God Himself.

Roberts uses Paul's thorn to explain "the thorn that God uses and the sickness that glorifies God." (Roberts, 1947, p. 52). He elaborates:

> The apostle Paul tells us of his "thorn in the flesh" (2 Cor 12:1-12). He says that it was given to him for two reasons: He had been caught up in the third heaven where he had abundant revelations. For this reason, his being a man, he was in danger of becoming proud and the people might give him more praise than he was worthy of. Hence, he says, "there was given to me a thorn in the flesh, the messenger of satan to buffet me, lest I should be exalted above measure."

> ... He says that this thing was so powerful that he "besought the Lord thrice that it might depart from me. And He said unto me, My grace is sufficient for thee: for my strength is made perfect in weakness. Most gladly therefore will I rather glory in my infirmities (weakness, marginal rendering), that the power of Christ may rest upon me. Therefore I take pleasure in infirmities, in reproaches, in necessities,

in persecutions, in distresses (straits) for Christ's sake; for when I am weak, I am strong."

Paul prayed three times, God answered each time by saying "No," which meant He had a better and happier way. He reminded Paul that "My strength is made perfect in weakness." (Roberts, 1947, p. 52-53)

I've found this really is true. "The sickness that glorifies God is the one He does not feel best to heal but that give way to a greater miracle to serve a larger purpose" (Roberts, 1947, p. 55). Our aches and pains become instruments to keep us humble and dependent on God.

## Gratitude in That Toe-Stub

Dr. Paul Brand, in his book co-authored with Philip Yancey, *The Gift of Pain*, says, "If I held in my hands the power to eliminate physical pain from the world, I would not exercise it." (Brand, 1997, p. 219)

Why would a physician, who pledged to prescribe only beneficial treatments, according to his abilities and judgment; to refrain from causing harm or hurt; and to live an exemplary personal and professional life as found in the Hippocratic Oath Code of Ethics, say something like this?

While working with leprosy patients in India and the United States, Brand became convinced that pain truly is one of God's greatest gifts to us.

I'll let him explain why in his own words:

Pain is actually a great benefactor to humankind, a gift

from God, not a curse, which allows us to know what needs to be done when we hurt ... such conditions as leprosy, diabetes, alcoholism, multiple sclerosis, nerve disorders, and spinal cord injury can also bring about the strangely hazardous state of insensitivity to pain. Ironically, while most of us see out pharmacies and doctors in search of relief from pain, these people live in constant peril due to pain's absence. I first learned about painlessness while working with leprosy, a disease that afflicts more than 12 million people worldwide. (Brand, 1997, pp. 5-6)

His extensive research discovered that it was not the "leprosy" which caused the disfigurement, it was the complete lack of pain around the injury. The lack of sensation would cause the victim to have serious infections that could not be felt. These infections would get worse, leaving a fingerless hand or foot which eventually had to be amputated.

Therefore, a leper's absence of pain was not a blessing, but rather a curse which allowed him to burn his hands or feet without realizing it; or even walk on raw wounds that could not be felt.

Dr. Brand concluded that pain is actually a great benefactor to humankind, a gift from God, not a curse, which lets us to know when to seek medical help.

Could it be at times the answer is, "No," so we can search and find, in our own soul, that the way to serve Him best is found in the willingness to serve Him through those who cannot do it for themselves? Is His answer, "No," part and portion of an awakening in ourselves to yearn and receive His Holy Spirit to be used to help others?

69

Is it fair to ask, "Why," when, despite the tens of thousands of miracles and healings God used Smith Wigglesworth to perform, his own daughter remained deaf? Will we get an answer from Him when we plead, "Why" do women suffer miscarriage after miscarriage, while others, desperately wanting a child, remain childless, too?

Do I dare ask Him, "Why" do I remain profoundly hearing impaired while He uses my mouth and my fingers to spread the Word of His Eternal Salvation? Would I approach His Holy Throne to bother Him to find out, "Why" does he find me worthy enough and love me so much that He uses me to participate in His wonderous miracles of healing?

I have come to know it's not important to know why. He knows and that is enough for me.

Perhaps it would be beneficial to consider this: When we break a bone, is God right there with us, reminding us through the pain to be a little more "still" while He mends it back together?

Imagine, He is that close to us in our pain! When our fever spikes, do we stop and realize that in His unfathomable brilliance, He's actually burning away the illness? Glory!

I know this for certain: God is trustworthy. He is steadfast. He is merciful. He loves me. He loves you.

His timing is always perfect. Sister Naomi, and my Mom, were right.

Trust His answers. His Holy Spirit is with us and never fails us. He hears our prayers – every single one of them.

# *Chapter Eight*

## He Hears Our Prayers

*"God is greater than our heart, and he knows everything."*

*(1 John 3:20)*

### He Knows the Maps of Our Hearts

God promised the Holy Spirit would be with us all the time. "I will ask the Father, and He will give you another Helper, that He may be with you forever" (John 14:16). Yet, there are times we wonder where He is ...

In the Garden of Gethsemane, the night before He was betrayed, Jesus prayed and heard God say, "No." Knowing what He would be enduring, the pain, the anguish, and torture of the cross, He cried out, "Abba, Father, everything is possible for you. Take this cup from me. Yet not what I will, but what you will" (Mark 14:36). Sweating blood, he pleaded this not once, but three times. And yet, God refused to take the cup away, and Jesus submitted to His Father's will.

Jesus knew there was no other way, God the Father said no to Jesus because of the importance of the mission, the fulfillment of the plan for salvation. There was no other way. It didn't make the thought of the reality that was about to occur any less frightening or agonizing. Jesus knew if mankind were to be forgiven, He would have to bear the full pain of the cross.

There isn't any other way to get to heaven except through Jesus (John 14:6; Acts 4:12). Had there been any other way, Jesus' heart wrenching request would have been granted, and He would have escaped the cruelty of the cross.

God knows the outcome even when we can't see it. Having faith that God is good and faithful means trusting Him in every situation, continuing to pray and maintain hope even when it seems impossible or hopeless. When the going gets rough, I find myself being strengthened by the promise in Romans 8:28, "And we know that God causes all things to work together for good to those who love God, to those who are called according to His purpose."

This life-changing moment comes to mind:

> Midafternoon sunlight streaming through the stain-glass windows, I was practically alone in the little perpetual adoration chapel. There were a handful of ancient sisters sitting quietly in the surrounding pews. It was quiet and peaceful and I began my silent prayer. Dear Jesus Lord, keep my children safe, unbreak their hearts, heal them, heal me ... please ... please

> I nodded off, at least I thought I did. When I opened my eyes, I was sitting at a table at an outdoor cafe, a huge umbrella covering the whole table shielding it from the hot summer sun. I looked up and saw I was having lunch with Jesus. I sat up straight, looking

down to make sure I was decently buttoned up.

A beggar approached our table. He was unkempt and dirty, bones protruding through his very soiled tattered garment. I reached to give him some food from my plate.

Jesus commanded, "No, don't do that!"

Startled, I looked up and said to Jesus, "but he's hungry! Didn't You tell us to feed the hungry, give drink to the thirsty, clothe the naked, visit the imprisoned?" ... I rattled off the corporal works of mercy straight from the Book of Matthew describing His own words from His Sermon on the Mount. Then, I realized I was arguing with our Lord and Master Jesus Himself! I was embarrassed and stopped talking. I felt my face blush.

Jesus said softly, "Do not give him anything."

Totally confused, I asked Him, "I don't understand. Why not?"

Jesus said, "Because that's Satan. If you give him even the smallest piece of anything, he will keep coming back for more and more until there is nothing left of you."

I was trying to do the right thing, the holy thing, following His holy directions and I realized I had it all wrong! Thoughts swirled. I was caught off-guard, out of context, in a different dimension. I looked up at Him and asked, "How do I know when to give and who to give it to?"

"Trust Me," was His answer.

Immediately, I was delivered wide awake back to the wooden pew. I searched the chapel and thought loudly: Wait! Wait! Don't go! Where are you?

I realized, at that moment, I had no idea how to trust Him. I had no idea what it meant to trust Him. During my life, I had prayed, I performed the works of mercy, I had taught my children how to pray, I had gone to church religiously and yet here I was, completely baffled. (Krueger and Nelson, 2019, *A Few Words on Your Identity in Christ*, p. 36)

I realized at that moment, even though I thought I had trusted Him, I truly wasn't trusting Him at all and I had no idea what this really meant or how to do it! Oh, I had been kidding myself, the reality was clear; I had no idea. I looked around, searched for Him, silently in my heart pleading for Him to return to tell me how to trust Him! I needed to know!

My "lunch" with Him that day changed my outlook. I realize now I was not alone during the long years I spent searching for Him to give me an answer. He was answering me with every breath I took, with every step I was taking moving toward Him. I truly think everyone goes through a time like I did, wanting to know if He's real, searching for answers. It's that ubiquitous "why" reverberating in our souls, our spirits, the universe, begging an answer. The spiritual desert is not a land of punishment; truly, it's a place of discovery, refreshment, refinement of the soul.

The Book of Isaiah (35:1-10 paraphrased) says:

> "The desert shall rejoice and blossom," says Isaiah,
> "For waters shall break forth in the wilderness,
> and streams in the desert;
> the burning sand shall become a pool,
> and the thirsty ground springs of water."

Blogger Adam Thomas puts it this way,

> When Abraham and Sarah, our great spiritual ancestors, left home and started wandered [*sic*] the hot sands, they discovered an astounding thing. God was there in the desert. When the ancient Israelites escaped Egypt and spent forty years wandering the land, they discovered an amazing truth. God was there in the desert. When I'm brought up short and realize I'm in the midst of a spiritual dry spell, the only way to keep existing, to keep from shriveling up completely, is to remember this truth. God is there in the desert. God transforms our spiritual deserts into new fertile lands. We cannot make this transformation ourselves; we can only participate in God's movement, which changes our parched landscapes into places where there is abundant blossoming.
>
> Oftentimes it is spiritual dryness that leads to spiritual growth. The dry spell returns to us the seeker's heart that we had lost. We gain new affinity for others who are struggling through their own droughts, spiritual or otherwise. We find new reserves of compassion and empathy. (Thomas, 2017, Retrieved from: https://

wherethewind.com/2016/12/12/the-spiritual-desert/)

We find our answer, we arrive at a holy place where we know God better, because His HOLY SPIRIT is with us; because we love Him and search for Him, He works within us for our betterment and His Glory (Romans 8:28).

So, how did I learn to trust Him? Was it an automatic thing, one day in the desert I woke up and just knew? No. This search took years for me. I cried and even threw a few tantrums. I came to the point where I realized I can't comprehend God or His ways – no one can. Little Miss Know-It-All had to concede – however; what a magnificent concession it was! I came to know, in His care, everything would be alright. He reminds us in His Word: "My thoughts are not your thoughts, neither are your ways my ways" (Is. 55:8). It may not take you as long. God's timing is always perfect.

We cannot even begin to guess God's thoughts, His motives, or His strategies. All we can do is trust Him and pray. He tells us to tell Him what we want and need, while assuring us that we will be able to accept that whatever His will is for us, in the long run, will be the best for us. That can be very hard at the time of prayer, but that's where faith comes in.

Someday, I am confident I'll be able to finish that lunch with Jesus. I've learned the power there is in the virtue of patience. I'll also have the chance to find out the "why" behind so many other confusing events in my life. Until then, I'll keep praying and I'll keep trusting in Him, because I know He is with me all the time in His Holy Spirit. I know He loves me – He loves you, too, very much and in His care, all will work out for our good and His Glory – and I am more than alright with that.

There are times we feel our prayers and cries to God aren't being heard because we are not seeing a change in our situations. This is one of the enemy's favorite lies; nothing is farther from the truth, really. We are to put all our trust into God's hands, after all, "God is greater than our heart, and he knows everything" (1 John 3:20). Just because we do not see an immediate change doesn't mean God has not heard us, because He hears each one of us loud and clear!

## Do What God Tells You to Do.

Pray and follow directions. I asked a Roman Catholic Sister of Mercy, "How do we know what God's will for us is?" She smiled that special nuns-always-know-the-answer smile and said, "Well, you know what isn't His will, so don't do that thing, and do the next right thing instead." Of course, she was right. Short, simple nun-answers often are the best ones.

R. T. Kendall has a word or two to say about obedience:

> "So he did what the LORD had told him" (1 Kings 17:5). Obedience. This is the secret: Doing what God tells you to do. Nothing more; just do it. He went to the Kerith Ravine, east of the Jordan, and stayed there." He stayed there. You do not move until God says to move. You stay there. It is the way the children of Israel were guided in the wilderness: "Whenever the cloud lifted from above the tabernacle, they would set out; but if the cloud did not lift, they did not set out – until the day it lifted" (Exodus 40:36-37). (Kendall, 2013, p. 32)

Jesus directly commanded that we obey Him as an expression of our love for Him. It isn't that we can earn God's love for us, but that the overflow of our love for Him is manifested in our following His directions. We *want* to obey Him because we love Him. We know, "He first loved us" (John 14:9). John 14:23 says, "Jesus answered and said to him, 'Whoever loves me will keep my word, and my Father will love him, and we will come to him and make our dwelling with him.'"

Once again, Philip Yancey has just the right words,

> One who has been touched by grace will no longer look on those who stray as "those evil people" or "those poor people who need our help." Nor must we search for signs of "love-worthiness." Grace teaches us that God loves because of who God is, not because of who we are. (Yancey, 1997, p. 280)

Obedience is born in our gratitude to God for His blessings, mercy, and grace. Our spiritual growth is impossible without the power of God. Holiness happens when we seek a fullness in our knowledge of Him, in our love for Him, in our obedience to Him. John 14:21 says, "Whoever has my commandments and keeps them, he it is who loves me. And he who loves me will be loved by my Father, and I will love him and manifest myself to him."

When we obey God, we are acting in love, holiness, and humility. John 4:23-24 reminds us, "But the hour is coming, and is now here, when the true worshipers will worship the Father in spirit and truth, for the Father is seeking such people to worship him. God is spirit, and those who worship him must worship in spirit and truth."

## His Timing Is Always Perfect

Jesus said, "Ask and it will be given to you; seek and you will find; knock and the door will be opened to you" (Matthew 7:7). R. T. Kendall explains:

> The Greek tense in these verbs shows that we ask but *we keep on asking*; we seek but *we keep on seeking*; we knock and *we keep on knocking*. Jesus taught that we should never, never, never give up when it comes to prayer (see Luke 18:1). I cannot begin to describe how much this verse and this concept mean to me. There are items on my prayer list that I was asking and praying about years ago. I refuse to give up. Seven times Elijah said to his servant, "Go back." Keep watching. God is never too early, never too late, but always just on time. "The Seventh time the servant reported, 'A cloud as small as a man's hand is rising from the sea'" (1 Kings 18:44). (Kendall, 2013, p. 106)

Don't give up, don't give in. I often remember what Jesus said at lunch when I wanted to give part of my lunch to the beggar,

> Jesus said, "Because that's Satan. If you give him even the smallest piece of anything, he will keep coming back for more and more until there is nothing left of you." (Krueger and Nelson, 2019, p. 36)

He said, "nothing left of you!" not, nothing left **for** you! There would be nothing left **of** you! He wasn't talking about it taking the rest of my lunch, JESUS was talking about the enemy stealing my very soul, little by little, by sin, until there was nothing left of me!

I was trying to do the right thing, the holy thing, following His holy directions and I realized I had it all wrong! Thoughts swirled. I was caught off-guard, out of context, in a different dimension. I looked up at Him and asked, "How do I know when to give and who to give it to?"

"Trust Me," was His answer. (ibid.)

Yes, Lord, I trust you now! I get it!

Our struggles become the very thing that glorifies the Lord. 1 Peter 1:6-7 tells us, "In all this you greatly rejoice, though now for a little while you may have had to suffer grief in all kinds of trials. These have come so that the proven genuineness of your faith – of greater worth than gold, which perishes even though refined by fire – may result in praise, glory and honor when Jesus Christ is revealed." (DeGarmo, 2019, Retrieved from: https://www.crosswalk.com/faith/women/what-we-need-to-remember-when-god-says-no.html)

"In their hearts humans plan their course, but the Lord establishes their steps" (Proverbs 16:9).

"There is a time for everything, and a season for every activity under the heavens" (Ecc 3:1).

I learned in that spiritual desert:

> It is the Holy Spirit who moves back and forth, bringing communication from our hearts to God and from God's heart to us. He is accustomed to striving with men's hearts. When you feel a craving and a desire to be more like God and live a holy life, that is

the moving and the functioning of the Holy Spirit on your behalf. (Sumrall, 1982, p. 21)

Even the apostle Thomas wandered around wondering. He doubted Jesus had returned from the dead; yet, he received the Holy Spirit in his state of contrition. I think if we're all honest with ourselves, we all have doubts from time to time. Then, there He is, smiling broadly right into our hearts, putting us back together with His grace when we're not even looking.

Oh, we can pretend everything is alright and we don't need Him, like the old-time game show participants who said they had perfect families and perfect marriages and perfect houses. Truth is, no one is perfect except Him, and even He almost gave His earthly parents heart failure when He went missing at the age of twelve. Mary and Joseph found Him in the temple preaching. Natch. Well, actually un-natch. He was – and is God. And He is with us now through His Holy Spirit.

Trust Him. He always was and always will be. He is all-knowing and everlasting. He is forever.

# *Chapter Nine*

## The Holy Spirit Always Is Everywhere

*In the beginning God created the heavens and the earth.*
*The earth was formless and void,*
*and darkness was over the surface of the deep,*
*and the Spirit of God was moving over the surface of the waters.*

*(Genesis 1:1-2)*

God knows everything about you. He created you. You are His masterpiece:

> For You created my innermost parts;
> You wove me in my mother's womb.
> I will give thanks to You, because I am awesomely
> and wonderfully made;
> Wonderful are Your works,
> And my soul knows it very well.
> My frame was not hidden from You
> When I was made in secret,
> And skillfully formed in the depths of the earth;
> Your eyes have seen my formless substance;
> And in Your book were written
> All the days that were ordained for me,

When as yet there was not one of them. (Psalm
139:13-16)

What does it mean we are created in God's image? Well, for one
thing, we have "forever" souls that will never die.

> At an appointed time in history, the Son of God
> stepped into His creation taking on the form of a man
> (Philippians 2:7). He added humanity without losing
> deity. Scripture also reveals that God is Spirit (John
> 4:24). It would appear that taking on a human body
> is part of what has given Jesus the ability to relate
> with human beings rather than it being an attribute of
> God as a display of His image. John tells us that Jesus
> became flesh to show us God's glory (John 1:14). This
> is the glory that mankind was meant to reflect when we
> were created in God's image.

> Other Scriptures would suggest that a human body is
> not essential to image bearing. It would be difficult to
> suggest that the disembodied souls under the throne
> in Revelation 6:9–11 have ceased to be image bearers
> on the basis that they are awaiting their resurrection
> bodies. Perhaps the same may be considered for
> Moses and Elijah who were talking with Jesus at the
> transfiguration (Matthew 17:1–3).

> This is not to say that the human body should not
> be highly valued. God created Adam and Eve with
> bodies, and their bodies were part of His "very good"
> creation. In Christ, our bodies are the temple of
> the Holy Spirit (1 Corinthians 6:19) and we are to

> use them as instruments of righteousness (Romans
> 6:12–13). (Ham, 2015, Retrieved from: https://
> answersingenesis.org/genesis/what-is-image-of-
> god/)

We are here on this earth for a short time, our loving Creator offers us the opportunity to spend eternity with Him. He is always with us:

> God's promise that "I will never leave you nor forsake
> you" is found in multiple books of the Bible, in both
> the Old and New Testaments. With this promise,
> we can be assured that He is always with us and
> encouraged to always be with God in faith and spirit.
> No matter our past, we can always repent and return
> to God's loving mercy and grace. Let us give thanks
> for God's glorious love and compassion for us. (Staff
> at BibleStudy Tools, 2020, Retrieved from: https://
> www.biblestudytools.com/topical-verses/i-will-
> never-leave-you-nor-forsake-you/)

## The Holy Spirit Is Omnipotent and Ubiquitous

Since the Holy Spirit is the very Spirit of God, He always was, and always will be. When He created us, He gave us the gift of free will. We have the blessed opportunity to decide to invite His Holy Spirit into our lives. Smith Wigglesworth says this about the Holy Spirit in his book, *On Healing*:

> I want to say to you believers that there is a very
> blessed place for you to attain to, and the place where
> God wants you is a place of victory. When the Spirit of

87

the Lord comes into your life, there must be victory. The disciples, before they received the Holy Spirit, were always in bondage ... However, beloved, after they received the power of the outpouring of the Holy Spirit, they were made bold as lions to meet any difficulty. They were made to stand any test ... They were bold. What made them like this? Purity. I tell you, purity is bold. Take for instance, a little child. He will gaze straight into your eyes for as long as you like, without looking away once. The purer a person is, the bolder he is. I tell you, God wants to bring us into that divine purity of heart and life, that holy boldness. Not arrogance, not big-headedness, but a pure, holy, divine appointment by One who will come in and live with you. He will defy the powers of satan and put you in a place of victory, a place of overcoming the world. (Wigglesworth, 1999, p. 137)

When we make that decision to accept His Holy Gift to us, when we invite the Holy Spirit into our life through Baptism in the Spirit, extraordinary changes occur.

When people think of baptism, they generally think only about Baptism by Water (Romans 3:23-24; Mk 1:4-5; Acts 4:41; 8:12; 36-38), and do not know about Baptism in the Spirit. John the Baptist had this to say about Baptism in the Holy Spirit:

In the Book of Matthew, we read John the Baptist saying, "I baptize you with water for repentance, but one who is more powerful than I is coming after me; I am not worthy to carry his sandals. He will baptize you with the Holy Spirit and fire" (Matthew 3:11) John the Baptist is referring to the ministry works of the coming Messiah.

In the Book of Mark, John the Baptist says the following. "I baptize you with water, but he will baptize you with the Holy Spirit" (Mark 1:8) using the exact same phrase Matthew remembers.

Luke remembers John the Baptist's words this way, "John answered them all, 'I baptize you with water, but one more powerful than I am is coming–I am not worthy to untie the strap of his sandals. He will baptize you with the Holy Spirit and fire'" (Luke 3:16). Luke is making the same prediction about the coming Messiah as Matthew and Mark.

The Apostle John, the evangelist of the group, records the words of John the Baptist as the one who spoke of the person who will "baptize with the Holy Spirit." "I myself did not know him, but the one who sent me to baptize with water said to me, 'He on whom you see the Spirit descend and remain is the one who baptizes with the Holy Spirit'" (John 1:33).

The only recorded time Jesus Christ used the phrase is found in the Book of Acts. Before His ascension into heaven Jesus said the following to His disciples. "John baptized with water, but in just a few days you will be baptized with the Holy Spirit" (Acts 1:5).

You see, baptism by water is separate and different from Baptism in the Holy Spirit.

## The Light of Life

I asked my dear friend, Pastor Verissa, to describe her own Baptism in the Spirit, and here's what she said:

Our Bible tells us that he who believes and is baptized

will be saved. Jesus told us to follow Him and He said greater things than these shall you do than I have done (John 14:12). The Book of Acts tells us about the twelve in the Upper Room that were left in one heat, one mind, one accord. They heard the mighty wind of God blowing through and saw the tongues of fire dancing on each one's head (Acts 2:3). The Bible tells us this gift is for every man, woman and child from generation to generations. Who am I to disagree with it? When I stood up to be baptized with the Holy Spirit they told me to sit down. The preacher kept preaching about the gift. The congregation told me to sit down and hush. The third time I stood up I turned to the congregation and asked how many wanted this gift from God. I am quite bold. Nineteen other people stood up, so I put my arm out and said give me the gift, knowing nothing from God will hurt me. I don't need to understand it, I need to accept it. There are many scriptures in the Bible and it's the Father and the Son who we ask to fill us with the precious Holy Spirit. I view the Word of God very simply yet deeply. The Trinity: God thinks it, Jesus speaks it and the Holy Spirit does it. (Nelson, 2016, p. 3)

There are a few things I think you should know about Pastor Verissa. She is the author of the Bible Systematic Theology Syllabus used by many congregations and missions around the world. Rick Renner asked Verissa if he could take her Syllabus to Russia when he was called to move there, and of course she said yes. It is used there to this day. Jose Murillo uses it in Latin America. It's used in South Korea and Brazil.

Some of Verissa's friends include Derek Prince, the Renner family, Joe and Linda Knight, Al Houghton, the Wilkerson brothers, and Leila Cost. She is emphatic in reporting that none of them had an influence on her life. They just became good friends at revivals. She told me, "Whenever they needed someone who walked in the Holy Spirit's gift of Miracles, they called me." God has used Pastor Verissa to start over 700 missions world-wide. She won't tell you this, though. She gets a kick out of saying her name is not on anything except her utility bill in Alaska.

How did she come upon this boldness in the Holy Spirit?

Jesus Christ visited her – twice.

## Comforter, Counselor, Advocate

Several decades ago, after suffering through a treacherous childhood, Verissa escaped from the house of her youth. Unable to read or write, she found her way to the West Coast, finding work in a strip club. Young and gorgeous, she worked her way to Anchorage where money and men were plentiful. Her life was tatted together with drugs and alcohol to get her through the day as a prostitute. There, she managed three strip clubs for the Mafia while servicing well-known visitors at the brothel, on-call.

In her early 30s, sick and tired of feeling sick and tired, with no real hope of any decent future, she decided to take her life by her own hand. Here's what happened:

> I was high and drunk, screaming at this person called Jesus, God. I used every foul word you could think of and told him all he wanted was people's money. I did my hair and make-up. I dressed myself in a white

91

peignoir flowing with ostrich feathers. I laid my head down on two pillows because I didn't want my sister to find my brains splattered on the walls. I put a .357 gun in my mouth and cocked the trigger. The room completely filled with what I thought was smoke but it smelled like lilac. I attempted to pull the trigger and a hand came between the trigger and the bullet. In the wrist of the hand was a hole and a voice said now you belong to me, you are mine. The man standing over me was Jesus. I jumped up and started screaming at the top of my lungs as loud as I could "Jesus is real, Jesus is real!" All the girls that worked at Eadie's came running into my room and fell to the floor on their faces the minute they hit the door. Little did I know then that He had delivered me from all my drug addictions, my alcoholism, my epilepsy, and dyslexia. I got up, got dressed, walked down to my motor home with the Glory of God still on my body, left everything behind except the clothes on my back. Took my purse, drove 25 miles to Sterling, AK. The glory lifted from my body, I figured this must be where He wants me. I parked at the Moose River campgrounds and stayed there. No money, no food, no clothes, just the Master, myself and Celeste, my sister. (Nelson, 2016, p.10)

I am convinced God loves us so much He is willing to do anything to help us when we ask. He knows the maps of our hearts.

He intercedes for us as our Comforter in times of need and our Counselor when we need direction (John 14:26-28), our Advocate when no one else is there for us (1 John 2:1). Believe

Him when He tells you He loves you. Have the faith of a child, for "faith is the assurance of things hoped for, the conviction of things not seen" (Hebrews 11:1).

*Do you not know that you are a temple of God and that the Spirit of God dwells in you? If anyone destroys the temple of God, God will destroy that person; for the temple of God is holy, and that is what you are.*

*(1 Cor. 3:16-17)*

*Chapter Ten*

## Believe

*Ears to hear and eyes to see—*
*both are gifts from the LORD.*
*(Proverbs 20:12)*

## Faith v. Feelings

Sister Briege McKenna is a Roman Catholic nun walking in the Holy Spirit's gifts of healings and miracles. She had been miraculously healed from rheumatoid arthritis when she was 24 years old. Seven years after she was healed, she wrote a book, *Miracles Do Happen: The Inspiring True Story of The World-Famous Healer and The Reality of Miracles*. It has been translated into many languages since, capturing the attention and the spiritual imaginations of countless pilgrims. I was one of them.

Heartbroken, financially ruined, and spiritually bankrupt in 1992, in the wake of my upended life, I found her book at a garage sale. I could not put it down until I'd finished it. Mind you, I was not looking for any answers, and I certainly was not looking for that book. I'd never heard of her and I wasn't in a very good

95

mood. Nonetheless, I was captivated by the back cover on the book which said:

> Sister Briege McKenna believes in the reality of miracles because she sees them happen. Since 1970, when she was healed of crippling arthritis, Sister Briege has experienced more of the extraordinary ways of the Spirit than most Christians ever imagine. (McKenna, 1987, back cover)

I was intrigued.

You see, I was raised to believe Miracles and Healings no longer really happened except in special, extremely rare circumstances, and only when a priest or high-up clergy was involved, certainly involving only extremely holy people, and mostly occurring after the intervention of dead people who were proving their worthiness to be canonized a real, true saint, end of story. Oh – and they need to rack up three posthumous miracles on earth to be worthy to be canonized a saint.

I figured Sister Briege was given special dispensation by the Pope to do these things, especially since most of the miracles involved the healing of ailing priests. Something nagged at me, though. What about her own healing, the one from rheumatoid arthritis? A recent blood panel had indicated I would end up suffering from the same thing someday, so I approached the book with a somewhat selfish agenda sprinkled with curiosity as to why this nun had these powers. Maybe she was sleeping with a bishop. No, it would have to be someone higher-up. A Cardinal. I was going to find out, whatever it was. I had spent the previous two years begging for a miracle. Clearly, God didn't know me well enough or He was busy with more pressing issues on more important people than me – or so I thought ...

Please understand, I mean no disrespect. This is what I was taught, and this is what I believed. I also was obedient and didn't read the Bible because I was taught not to, I was told I would learn everything I needed to know about God's Word from the readings at Mass – AND if I had any further questions, I could always ask a priest. Alrighty then. Back to Sister Briege ...

I am going to cut through the chase to the end game: Sister Briege unlocked the door to the Truth for me. There was nothing unholy or unsavory about her. She wasn't sleeping with anyone. It was clear God was using her; she was magnificently filled with His Holy Spirit and was glorifying Him with each and every miracle.

My own conversion onto the road to discipleship in Jesus Christ was initiated by His servant, Sister Briege McKenna, back in 1994 when I picked up her book at a garage sale (and I don't even like garage sales) and read it. Glory! Thank you, Jesus! I would be baptized in the Holy Spirit years later.

Sister Briege says,

> Being a Christian means you have made a commitment to follow Jesus Christ, to live according to His teachings and obey His commandments. Today, throughout the world, we are experiencing a renewal of faith. People are accepting Jesus for the first time or they are renewing faith in Him and their commitment to Him. (McKenna, 1987, p. 121).

Thank you, Sister! This marked the beginning of a long, arduous, yet joy-filled journey for me as His disciple. I went from being intrigued to being saved. After reading her book, I was changed. Transformed. I learned about real faith from that marvelous little book. I began to read His Word.

Sister McKenna added,

> Faith and feelings are two different things. There is no place in the word of God where Jesus said, "By your feelings you will be saved" or "By your feelings you will be healed." He did commend people on their faith. Faith is believing in what we don't see. Jesus said, "Blessed are those who do not see and yet believe." (McKenna, 1987, p. 61-62)

Kenneth Hagin agrees, and says in his blog titled, "Faith vs. Feelings":

> Central Truth: A formula for faith is: (1) Find a promise in God's Word for whatever you are seeking, (2) Believe God's Word, (3) Do not consider contradictory circumstances, and (4) Praise God for the answer.

> The beloved man of faith, Smith Wigglesworth, once said, "I can't understand God by feelings. I can't understand the Lord Jesus Christ by feelings. I can only understand God the Father and Jesus Christ by what the Word says about them. God is everything the Word says He is. We need to get acquainted with Him through the Word." Too many people try to get acquainted with God through their personal feelings. When they feel good, they think God has heard their prayers. If they don't feel particularly good they

think He has not heard them. Their faith is based on their feelings whereas it should be based on God's word. (Hagin, 2017, Retrieved from: https://www.hopefaithprayer.com/faith/kenneth-hagin-faith-lesson-no-7-faith-vs-feelings/)

In the summer of 1922, Smith Wigglesworth wrote a chapter in one of his many books and called it, "Faith that Leads to the Treasures of God." In it, he says:

> I believe the Lord would be magnified and pleased if we are to continue our subject we   had yesterday morning from the 11th chapter of Hebrews. I will read the first verse,

> Now faith is the substance of things hoped for, the evidence of things not seen. For by it the elders obtained a good report. Through faith we understand that the worlds were framed by the word of God, so that things which are seen were not made of things which do appear. By faith Abel offered unto God a more excellent sacrifice than Cain, by which he obtained witness that he was righteous, God testifying of his gifts: and by it he being dead yet speaketh. By faith Enoch was translated that he should not see death; and was not found, because God had translated him: for before his translation he had this testimony, that he pleased God. But without faith it is impossible to please him: for he that cometh to God must believe that he is, and that he is a rewarder of them that diligently seek him. By faith Noah, being warned of God of

things not seen as yet, moved with fear, prepared an ark to the saving of his house; by which he condemned the world, and became heir of the righteousness which is by faith. By faith Abraham, when he was called to go out into a place which he should after receive for an inheritance, obeyed; and he went out, not knowing whither he went. By faith he sojourned in the land of promise, as in a strange country, dwelling in tabernacles with Isaac and Jacob, the heirs with him of the same promise: For he looked for a city which hath foundations, whose builder and maker is God (Hebrews 11:1-10). (Wigglesworth, 2006, p. 53-54)

He concluded with, "I believe that there is only one way to all the treasures of God, and it is the way of faith." (ibid.)

## We Don't Have to Know Everything

I have to remind myself sometimes that wanting to know everything was Eve's downfall. She just *had* to know, didn't she? I used to be that way. We're seeing this in our society at large. The secularists say, "If science can't prove it, then it doesn't exist." Let's face a basic truth here. Some things in life are mysteries. Just because we can't see something, doesn't mean it doesn't exist. I know Tokyo exists even though I haven't been there. We know there is a planet named Mars even though we have not been there.

Knowledge is not power. Faith is. "When Jesus spoke again to the people, he said, 'I am the light of the world. Whoever follows me will never walk in darkness, but will have the light of life'" (John 8:12).

One of my favorite devotionals about this very thing is this one:

> Rise and shine, Buttercup! Turn on the lights! Get
> going! It's going to be a great day! Sure, sometimes
> it would be fabulous during a cold wintery phase of
> life to burrow deeper into the soft, feathery, warm
> down comforter of life and sleep some more. There's
> too much to do – but it can wait. Clients to see – but
> another day. Friendships to nurture – but they'll
> understand. Prayers to say – but He already knows I
> love Him. The excuses.
>
> The clock ticks away. It is not waiting for me or for you
> or for anyone. There are some things – like the Truth
> – that just can't be put off any longer. It's time to get
> up. Time to show up. Do you sleep in the dark Land
> of Excuses?
>
> The crowd turned a deaf ear to Jesus when He told
> them, "I am the Light of the world." The religious
> leaders were clueless what he meant because they
> were in a cold wintery phase of spiritual darkness.
> Even though they had the Law down pat, they didn't
> have the Light of life. They didn't understand what
> Jesus was talking about at all. Many people follow false
> teachings to this day that lead to ruin. Jesus Christ is
> the true Light of life. We must exercise due diligence
> with His word, submit ourselves to His teachings –
> even when we are too tired or too distracted. It's not
> enough to just see the glow from a distance, we have to
> train ourselves to seek His Light and follow it, exercise

walking in it and learn how to live it. Discipline and discipleship. Rise and shine!

I pray, Dear Lord God, Wake me up and teach me how to be Your disciple. Discipline me to get up, show up, lace up and turn on your Light of salvation in my life!

Sometimes, it's easier to pull the covers over our head. It takes gumption to put our foot down on the floor and plow through the day anyway. Once our eyes adjust to the Light of the day, the going gets easier. What are the excuses you make most often to avoid getting the tasks at-hand completed? When we suit up and show up, Christ is with us every step of the way. (Krueger and Nelson, 2018, p. 98)

## Ears to Hear, and Not the Ones You're Wearing

But He said, "More than that, blessed are those who hear the word of God and keep it!" (Luke 11:28)

My earthly ears don't work very well. I'm in the "severe to profound hearing loss" category on the audiology report I carry around with me. I have to show this paper sometimes to people to explain why I have a service dog in tow. Despite severely limited hearing, I'm able to carry on conversations provided there's not a lot of background noise and I am wearing a hearing device in my left ear. Even though my ears don't work, my heart listens attentively and hears the Word of God loud and clear. It wasn't always like that, though. The more I read and share His word, the stronger I am.

> God's word is sturdy, steady, true and life-changing. God gave us His Word to bless us. To listen means to "pay heed" – to have an attentive ear, to be quiet. To be blessed means to be "made holy" or "consecrated." To be truly blessed, we respond to the word of God, keep it in our hearts, share it and live it. (Krueger and Nelson, 2017a, p. 42)

It's not enough to just hear words being spoken, any more than it's enough to look at food on a plate and not eat it. We live the Word of God after we've heard it.

Three years ago, I met Dr. Gary Wood. He was a devoted evangelist preaching God's Word to whomever would listen. He had died in an automobile accident many years ago, back when he was in college. Pronounced legally and medically dead by the attending docs, little did they know he was spending twenty minutes in heaven having a conversation with God. God miraculously healed him and promised him that wherever he told his story, people would be saved, healed, and delivered. God sent him back, stunning everyone in the ER. He has seen God heal people of leukemia, cancer, blindness, arthritis, and many other infirmities. Thousands have been saved.

Dr. Wood explains it this way in his book, *Miracles, God's Heavenly Touch on Man*,

> Healing occurs after prayer has been offered and sometimes take time but there is continued improvement in health until perfect health manifests. Jesus did not promise everyone would receive a miracle but He did declare, "They shall recover" (Mark 16:18). A lot of people give up if they don't

receive a miracle. They believe God has not heard them. In many cases in the Bible, Jesus waited for faith to come to the sufferer's heart and they were willing to do whatever Jesus told them to do. Jesus often said, "According to your faith be it done unto you. (Wood, 2013, p. 78)

He continues,

To get faith you need to read the Bible and find God's promises to heal you. This may take time but God's word says in Roman's 10:17 that faith comes by hearing and hearing by the word of God. (ibid.)

Listen, listen with your heart. Is He calling you? Are you ready to say, "Yes!" yet?

# *Chapter Eleven*

## Yes, He is Here for You, Too

*As for you, the anointing which you received from Him abides in you, and you have no need for anyone to teach you; but as His anointing teaches you about all things, and is true and is not a lie, and just as it has taught you, you abide in Him.*

*(I John 2:27)*

## So, How Does This Happen?

The Apostles did not rush around laying hands on people to impart an experience of fire or power after they received the gift of the Holy Spirit on Pentecost (John 15:16-31). They did not chant words, nor did they expect healings and miracles, or other supernatural events following their Baptism in the Holy Spirit. They just KNEW God would work through each one of them for His Glory and their good (Romans 8:28) according to His will for them.

The Holy Spirit does exactly that for us – He comforts us, helps us, moves within our hearts to guide us, directs us and helps us when we open our hearts to Him.

The account of the woman touching the hem of the Lord's garment is a wonderful example of how He is here for us in our faith and love for Him. Hers is a story of immense faith; she had determined in her own mind that if she could only touch His clothing she would be healed. When Jesus felt her touch, he turned to her and said, "Take heart, daughter. Your faith has healed you!" (Matt. 9:22). It wasn't that His cloak held any power, it wasn't anything magical like Simon the Sorcerer thought it to be, rather, her faith was such that she believed that even touching what Jesus was wearing would heal her. And He did.

Often, miracles, healings, and other supernatural events are accompanied by the use of anointing with holy oil. God anointed some men and women in the Bible. If you're like me, you may be wondering, "What exactly is 'the anointing,' and how does one receive it?"

Since God can do whatever He wants to do whenever He wants to do it, a person can receive God's anointing in several ways. It can be taken away as quickly as it is given, too. A great example is this, found in the Book of Acts 19:11-12, which reads, "God did extraordinary miracles through Paul, so that even handkerchiefs and aprons that had touched him were taken to the sick, and their illnesses were cured and the evil spirits left them."

Here's what Denver Cheddie at Bibleissues.org has to say about anointing:

> But what is this anointing that is so much talked about today? To anoint means to smear on or to rub. In the Old Testament, people, animals, and objects were literally anointed or rubbed with oil. This was done for many purposes. Sheep were anointed to

protect them from blood sucking insects. A shield would be anointed to maintain its physical properties. Officials were anointed as a sign of consecration. In a different sense, anyone used by God for any purpose was referred to as God's anointed. This included prophets, priests, rulers and even pagan kings like Cyrus. Jesus is referred to as the Christ or the Anointed One. Thus the anointing was related in part to function performed as well as office held. In other words God anointed those whom He appointed.

Nowhere in the Bible is the anointing ever portrayed as a mystic force that sends people hurling to the floor, into convulsions, fits of hysterical laughter, or episodes of "holy rolling"; yet today these phenomena are readily attributed to the "anointing." (Cheddie, 2001, Retrieved from: https://bibleissues.org/anointing1.html)

The Anointing is the Power of God given to meet the needs of hurting humanity through His Holy Spirit. In the Beginning God gave His Authority, Power, and Anointing to Adam, to Noah, to Abraham, and to Moses and Joshua. The Power of His Holy Spirit has always been and always will be.

When a person invites God's Holy Spirit into their life, something happens – something takes place. This holy anointing can be felt. This is not an earthly phenomenon, rather, it is a supernatural event. It's about a person coming into contact with a living God – the Creator of heaven and earth whose Spirit is with us!  This power – this anointing – was promised to us by Jesus (Acts 1:8).

## Let's Talk More About Anointing

R. T. Kendall, pastor and best-selling author, explains it this way:

> The anointing, then, is the Holy Spirit. It is really just another word for the Holy Spirit. It is one of John's special words for the Spirit, "You have an anointing from the Holy One ... The anointing received from Him remains in you, and you do not need anyone to teach you" (1 John 2:20, 27). Because the Holy Spirit is our teacher, he "will teach you all things" and "will guide you into the truth" (John 14:26; 16:13).
>
> I would rather have more of this than anything. I want more of the Holy Spirit than I want anything in the world. In Proverbs the anointing is called "wisdom" and "understanding." "Wisdom is supreme; therefore get wisdom. Though it cost all you have, get understanding" (Proverbs 4:7). James uses this word wisdom: "If any of you lacks wisdom, he should ask God, who gives generously to all without finding fault, and it will be given to him" (James 1:5). (Kendall, 2003, p. 4, 5)

Kathryn Kuhlman, talks about Holy Spirit Anointing in "The Greatest Power in the World,"

> Being filled with the Holy Spirit, the experience we

call the baptism of the Holy Spirit, is a work that the Holy Spirit does in us, so that through us He might be a power for service. We cannot receive this all-important experience and not know it. We do not receive Baptism of the Holy Spirit, the infilling experience of the Holy Ghost, by faith – *we receive it by surrender.*

All right, what did Jesus say before He went away? He promised, "Ye shall receive power, after that the Holy Ghost is come upon you" (Acts 1:8), and you do not receive this power by faith. You do not receive this glorious dynamite, this magnificent dynamo, by faith. You do not come into contact with this glorious power by faith.

Let me explain. Look at the second chapter of the Book of Acts. As they tarried there in the upper room, they received nothing by faith. By faith they went into the upper room. By faith they accepted that which Jesus had promised. But their tarrying was mighty real, and when they came out of that upper room, not one of them had accepted that experience by faith. *Something really happened!* Was there an outward evidence of it? I told you before that when one is born again, there very definitely is an outward evidence. That person is a new creature in Jesus Christ and everyone will know it if you have truly been born again. In exactly the same way, there will be an outward evidence of the filling of the Holy Ghost if you have had that experience." (Kuhlman, 1997, p. 55)

So, we see that by faith we are healed – being filled with the Holy Spirit by baptism is different! There is the anointing. As Kendall pointed out, in Proverbs the anointing is called "wisdom" and "understanding." There is the anointing by the Holy Spirit – the very Spirit of God – which always was and always will be.

The foundational Scripture is found in Luke 4:14-19:

> Jesus returned to Galilee in the power of the Spirit, and news about him spread through the whole countryside. He was teaching in their synagogues, and everyone praised him.
>
> He went to Nazareth, where he had been brought up, and on the Sabbath day he went into the synagogue, as was his custom. He stood up to read, and the scroll of the prophet Isaiah was handed to him. Unrolling it, he found the place where it is written:
>
> "The Spirit of the Lord is on me,
> because he has anointed me
> to proclaim good news to the poor.
> He has sent me to proclaim freedom for the
> prisoners and recovery of sight for the blind,
> to set the oppressed free,
> to proclaim the year of the Lord's favor."

It is so very important to have an understanding of this anointing today – in the day and time that we are living. Many today do not recognize the power of God and need to be told.

Johnathon Doctor, from the Family Faith Ministries, explains this beautifully in his article, "The Transfer of Anointing":

I have the best news for those who desire to be used by God. That news is that the same anointing that was displayed in the ministry of Jesus is available to you as well. The Anointing is the Power of God given to meet the needs of hurting humanity. The Anointing is tangible, it is transferable. The Transfer of power, authority and anointing is available to you today. In the Beginning God transferred His Authority, Power and Anointing to Adam, to Noah, to Abraham and to Moses and Joshua. The Anointing was transferred down the line, Elijah, Elisha, Gideon, Sampson, David etc. Throughout Bible history we see the Anointing being transferred down from one generation to another, from one servant of God to another.

When Jesus walked on this earth He was anointed to heal, deliver and set men free from the works of the devil. Jesus went everywhere healing the sick, casting out devils, raising the dead and setting the captives free.

Before Jesus was taken up into heaven, He said that it was better that He went away so that the Holy Spirit could come. On the Day of Pentecost Jesus Transferred the Anointing that He had to His disciples. We see the same anointing that was operating in Jesus' ministry operating in those who believed.

Just like Elijah went away and Elisha received a double portion. Likewise, Jesus went away and the church received the same anointing, but this anointing was to do the works of Jesus and greater. This same anointing is not limited to just one physical body of Jesus but this Anointing has been transferred to all who believe. A double portion. Just like God anointed Jesus of Nazareth with the Holy Ghost and Power to go about to do good and heal all that were oppressed of the devil, to destroy the works of the enemy, so He has made that anointing available to you. First John 2:20 says that we have an anointing, vs. 27 says that anointing is in us. This burden removing yoke destroying anointing is in us. As we Receive the Baptism of the Holy Ghost, we too have received the transfer of this anointing for this generation. Just like we see the Anointing operating in Jesus, Peter, Paul, Phillip and Stevens life we can expect that same anointing to operate in our life and ministry as we Go in Jesus' Name. The law of Association works with the anointing as well. As we associate with the Word of God and one another the anointing will rub off on each other.

As we see this anointing operating in men and woman of our day, servants of God like Smith Wigglesworth, Charles Finney, Oral Roberts, Kenneth Hagin, Kenneth Copeland, Jerry Savelle etc. the Anointing to heal and deliver and set men free is here and available to your ministry. The purpose of this anointing is to Set the captives free and meet the needs of hurting humanity.

The Anointing was transferred by the way of the laying on of hands, by oil, by touch, by cloths, and by words. Every point of contact was by faith. Power and anointing is available to us in this generation. Miracle energy is available, the Ability of God is available. God needs us to be His "delivery boys" of His Anointing. God needs us to carry this Anointing to this generation.

114

Like electricity needs a breaker box to light up the house, we are that breaker box to transfer and bring the electricity of God's Power and Anointing to this generation, to bring Life and Love and Anointing to this hurting generation. Christ means Anointed One, and we are Christians, we are little Anointed ones.

The Anointing is not limited to Apostles or special select few, but to all who believe, to all who be willing to bring this anointing to others. (Doctor, 2019, From: www.fofmc.net)

## Anointing Is Tangible and It Is Transferrable

We see, the Anointing is tangible, and it is transferable. This glorious transfer of power, authority, and anointing is available to us today. Mark 16:15-18,20, John 14:12-14, Mark 11:22-24, and Acts 1:8 tell us this; the anointing of the Holy Spirit is available to us in this time - in all generations. Since the beginning, God transferred His Authority, Power, and Anointing to Adam, to Noah, to Abraham, and to Moses and Joshua. Here is a list of Scriptural evidence of this anointing:

Transfer of Anointing Scriptural Evidence:
Genesis 1:26; 6:8   Adam and Noah
Genesis 12:1-3     Abraham
Exodus 9:16,23 Exodus 14:21-22  Moses
Numbers 27:22-23  Moses to Joshua
Deut. 34:9  from Moses to Joshua
Joshua 3:7  Joshua
Joshua 6:2,5  Joshua 10:12-14  Joshua
Judges 6:34  Gideon
Judges 13:24-25  Judges 14:5-6;  15:14-15  Sampson

1 Samuel 16:13 from Samuel to David
1 Kings 17:17-24 Elijah
2 Kings chapters 2 through 13; 13:20-21 Elisha

## Yes, This Is for You, Too

Paul tells Timothy "And the things that you have heard from me among many witnesses, commit these to faithful men, who will be able to teach others also" (2 Timothy 2.2). Our spiritual growth is dependent on the testing of our faith, by our faithful reading of God's Word, and understanding how to live the Word in our lives daily.

The precious Gift of His Holy Spirit indwelling within us changes everything!

We are His. He is with us. Always.

# Chapter Twelve

## The Holy Spirit Always Was and Always Will Be

*"And as I began to speak, the Holy Spirit fell upon them just as it had upon us at the beginning. And I remembered the word of the Lord, how he had said, 'John baptized with water, but you will be baptized with the Holy Spirit.'"*

*(Acts 11:15-16)*

## Filled With the Holy Spirit

Tasha Cobbs Leonard, a contemporary gospel singer, is an amazingly gifted musician. Her single, "Your Spirit," has had over 128M – yes, million – views on YouTube. Since I am hearing impaired, I turn up the volume as loudly as it goes and play her gospel music often. I am certain every demon in a several-mile radius from my house flees because of her music and me singing along. Praise music transports our Spirits to the Throne of God Himself, the best place to be – ever. Here it is, if you are interested in being lifted into the Heavens: https://www.youtube.com/watch?v=BZT8jqsc8lQ

Here are the lyrics:

> Not by might. Not by power. By your spirit God Send
> your spirit God. You are the fire. We are the temple.
> You are the voice. We are your song. You are our
> God. We are your people. You are the light. We stand
> in awe. We stand in awe of you. Not by might. Not by
> power. By your spirit God. Send your spirit God. You
> called us out. Out of the darkness. Into your love, into
> your light. Grace upon grace. Beauty for ashes. You
> come to us. We come alive. We stand in awe of you.
> We stand in awe of you. Not by might. Not by power.
> By your spirit God. Send your spirit God. Breathe,
> come and breathe on us. Spirit breathe on us. We
> stand in awe of you. Not by might. Not by power. By
> your spirit. Send your spirit God. Breathe, come and
> breathe on us. Spirit breathe on us.

> (Music video by Tasha Cobbs Leonard performing
> "Your Spirit" (C) 2017 Capitol Christian Music
> Group, Inc.) (Leonard, 2017, Retrieved from:
> https://www.youtube.com/watch?v=BZT8jqsc8lQ)

Yes, "This is the word of the LORD to Zerubbabel: 'Not by
might nor by power, but by my Spirit,' says the LORD of hosts."
(Zechariah 4:6)

The powerful, omnipotent, ubiquitous Spirit of God – the Holy
Spirit – the Spirit who always was and always will be, the Helper,
the Comforter, the Teacher. Jesus told His disciples, after His
Resurrection, and before His glorious Ascension into Heaven: "I
tell you the truth: it is to your advantage that I go away, for if I do

not go away, the Helper will not come to you. But if I go, I will send him to you" (John 16:7).

Alistair Begg, from Ligonier Ministries, shares these interesting truths about the Holy Spirit. He says,

> You know that the Greek word translated here as "Helper" is "*parakletos*." In its technical form, it has a legal dimension; it refers to one who would be an advocate. In its wider context, it speaks of comfort, of protection, of counsel, and of guidance. Jesus also spoke of the Spirit as the Helper in John 14 and introduced Him as "the Spirit of truth" (14:17; 16:13).
>
> The Holy Spirit is one both with the Father and with the Son. In theological terms, we say that He is both co-equal and co-eternal. When we read the whole Upper Room Discourse, we discover that it was both the Father and the Son who would send the Spirit (John 14:16; 16:7), and the Spirit came and acted, as it were, for both of Them. So, the activity of the Spirit is never given to us in Scripture in isolation from the person and work of Christ or in isolation from the eternal will of the Father. Any endeavor to think of the Spirit in terms that are entirely mystical and divorced from Scripture will take us down all kinds of side streets and eventually to dead ends.
>
> The Holy Spirit was the agent of creation. In the account of creation at the very beginning of the Bible, we are told: "In the beginning, God created the heavens and the earth. The earth was without

form and void, and darkness was over the face of the deep. And the Spirit of God was hovering over the face of the waters" (Gen. 1:1-2). The Hebrew word translated as "Spirit" here is "*ruach*," which also can mean "breath." The "*ruach elohim*," "the Breath of the Almighty," is the agent in creation. It is not the immateriality of the Spirit that is in view here, but rather His power and energy; the picture is of God's energy breathing out creation, as it were, speaking the worlds into existence, putting the stars into space. Thus, when we read Isaiah 40:26 and the question is asked, "Who created these?" we have the answer in Genesis 1:2–the Spirit is the irresistible power by which God accomplishes His purpose. (Begg, 2019, Retrieved from: https://www.ligonier.org/blog/ five-truths-about-holy-spirit/)

God the Father's very Holy Spirit; He has the perfect loving heart, the everlasting comforting presence; He is the healer of broken bodies, the mender of broken hearts, the renderer of redemption through JESUS, through Whom we arrive at His Holy Throne.

He is Creator, King, and the Christ.

So, in faith, we come before Him and ask to be filled with His Holy Spirit, to be made whole, to be created completely in His image. How do we do this?

Dr. R. L. Bowen explains to us, in his book, *Altar Ministry Handbook, A Guide for Altar Workers,* just what to do:

When you meet a person at the altar who is born

again and indicates a desire to be filled with the Holy Spirit, you do not need to do a lot of teaching or elaborate explanation. Some might ask about the benefit of being filled with the Holy Spirit. Some might think they received it all at salvation. To be sure, the individual that is born again has the Holy Spirit residing within. The baptism with/in the Holy Spirit is a different dimension, a deeper, fuller walk with Jesus Christ through the Holy Spirit.

When we are baptized in/with the Holy Spirit, the Holy Spirit is allowed to live through us more fully. Acts 1:8 says, "But you shall receive power when the Holy Spirit has come upon you; and you shall be witnesses to Me in Jerusalem, and in all Judea and Samaria, and to the end of the earth." When we are filled/baptized with/in the Holy Spirit, we hear the voice of the Lord more clearly and in greater depth. Yes, we heard the call of the Spirit when we were born again and now He wants to take us deeper in our relationship with Him. (Bowen, 2008, p. 59-60)

Fuchsia Pickett answered the call of the Spirit and revealed:

It took some extreme circumstances in my life to the place where the Holy Spirit began to reveal Jesus to me and in me. I will never forget the first night the Spirit began to "divide asunder" the veil of the flesh between my soul and spirit. I began to see Jesus and understand His Word. The Holy Spirit became my teacher, and I started to receive His divine revelation.

(Pickett, 1997, back flap)

After Jesus saved her life, Pastor Verissa knew she was filled with His Holy Spirit, too:

> I realized as soon as I read Mark 16, even though I was a babe in Christ. I believed it. I spoke in new tongues like it says, I battled demons in His name, so I started praying for the sick. *I thought all Christians did it.* The Bible says these signs will follow those who believe. Miracles, signs, and wonders are for the believers. We see them in our church all the time, including raising the dead. (Nelson, 2016, From: Interview, Non-Published.)

## Say Yes

Baptized in the Holy Spirit, we receive the perfect amount of grace to open heaven's door just enough to allow His Holy Light to shine on us, shedding perfect amounts of wisdom understanding according to His will for us. There are holy times when it's enough to actually witness His Holy Magnificence, other times to feel spiritually sturdy enough to humbly ask for forgiveness when the mere thought of it, otherwise, would be impossible.

It is when we are at our weakest that He is the strongest for us (2 Cor 12:10). Then, there are those amazing times when He hands us the keys to unlock the doors of Heaven's Heart to be able to alleviate the suffering of others through Him, manifested in healings, miracles, and even bringing back the dead. There are other times when we know, truly know, exactly what to say because God has replaced our words with His Words. He loves us so very much. If people knew the Power He is willing to make available to them through Him, they would fall over.

I did.

He lets us into His Holy Place with even just a smidgeon of faith, the exact amount we need according to Him, to be able to eke out a holy life on this earth. Enough so we can spend eternity with Him. We come to know the Power of Father God, the Love of Jesus Christ His beloved Son, and the Creation and Comfort of His Holy Spirit.

His Holy Word tells us:

> Now concerning spiritual gifts, brothers and sisters, I do not want you to be unaware. You know that when you were pagans, you were led astray to the mute idols, however you were led. Therefore I make known to you that no one speaking by the Spirit of God says, "Jesus is accursed"; and no one can say, "Jesus is Lord," except by the Holy Spirit.

> Now there are varieties of gifts, but the same Spirit. And there are varieties of ministries, and the same Lord. There are varieties of effects, but the same God who works all things in all persons. But to each one is given the manifestation of the Spirit for the common good. For to one is given the word of wisdom through the Spirit, and to another the word of knowledge according to the same Spirit; to another faith by the same Spirit, and to another gifts of healing by the one Spirit, and to another the effecting of miracles, and to another prophecy, and to another the distinguishing

of spirits, to another various kinds of tongues, and to another the interpretation of tongues. But one and the same Spirit works all these things, distributing to each one individually just as He wills.

For just as the body is one and yet has many parts, and all the parts of the body, though they are many, are one body, so also is Christ. For by one Spirit we were all baptized into one body, whether Jews or Greeks, whether slaves or free, and we were all made to drink of one Spirit. (1 Cor 12:1-13)

Now you are Christ's body, and individually parts of it. And God has appointed in the church, first apostles, second prophets, third teachers, then miracles, then gifts of healings, helps, administrations, and various kinds of tongues. All are not apostles, are they? All are not prophets, are they? All are not teachers, are they? All are not workers of miracles, are they? All do not have gifts of healings, do they? All do not speak with tongues, do they? All do not interpret, do they? But earnestly desire the greater gifts. (1 Cor 12:27-31)

Trust Him. Remember, Jesus didn't immediately heal Lazarus. Mary and Martha couldn't yet understand that He was going to do something even greater! Raising Lazarus from the dead glorified God (John 11:1-44) and took His earthly ministry to an entirely new level.

We learn to trust Him. We trust Him with our life, our death, and everything in between.

## Moving in the Spirit

"But the Advocate, the Holy Spirit, whom the Father will send in my name, will teach you all things and remind you of everything I have said to you." (John 14:26 NIV)

I'd love to close with this lovely tribute to my Mother:

> I have a brother named Joseph and a sister named Elizabeth I've never met. They died before I was born.
>
> A young teenager, I found the death certificates while snooping through papers in my parent's unlocked safe. I was not supposed to know. The discovery explained much to me. Like, why my Mother baked so many birthday cakes when it wasn't anyone's birthday. Like, why my Mother was so overwhelmingly protective of us, my surviving siblings and me.
>
> I think we all have secret rituals that keep us tied together with the ones we've lost. It's a way to keep them alive somehow.
>
> Mother is an expert in the art of graceful losing. She's lost children, her husband and most recently, large parts of her memory. She is ninety years old and remembers every detail about how to bake her delicious lemon meringue pie. She does not, however, remember anything we've talked about two minutes earlier.
>
> Many years ago, I was unkind to her. Time passed, I grew up. Embarrassed and sorrowful, I apologized.

She immediately completely forgave me. We've talked nearly every day since then for the last twenty years. Mom taught me how to pray when I was a little girl. Her most recent solicited advice to me? I must continue to pray for my children. Don't give up on them, she says.

The Holy Spirit is at home in my Mother's heart as her Comforter. I truly believe the dementia is a blessing. She has lost so much and doesn't even realize she's lost it. She asks me if I've seen Dad lately and I tell her he's waiting for her in heaven. She seems to be happy about that. I will keep calling her, knowing the day will come when she will not remember me. I'll call her anyway. She is not lonely. She is very loved. Her heart knows this. Her Spirit lives this.

Now it is God who makes both us and you stand firm in Christ. He anointed us, set his seal of ownership on us, and put his Spirit in our hearts as a deposit, guaranteeing what is to come (2 Corinthians 1:21).

Dear Jesus Lord God Almighty, thank you for sending your Holy Spirit to Comfort us, to heal us, to protect us. Please fill us each with Your Holy Spirit so that we are your hands and feet and eyes and heart for our brothers and sisters (Romans 12:9-13) until you return again! Please continue to bless my Mother; all Mothers. Amen! (Krueger and Nelson, 2018, p.166)

Alistair Begg finishes his discourse with this powerful, revealing conclusion which I will share with you now in conclusion:

The Holy Spirit is the author of the Scriptures: Second Timothy 3:16 tells us, "All Scripture is breathed out by God. ..." The Greek word behind this phrase is *theopneustos*, which means "God-breathed." In creation, we have the Spirit breathing His energy, releasing the power of God in the act of creation. We have the same thing in the act of redemption, and we see it again in the divine act of giving to us the record in the Scriptures themselves. The doctrine of inspiration is entirely related to the work of God the Holy Spirit. Peter affirms this view, writing, "No prophecy was ever produced by the will of man, but men spoke from God as they were carried along by the Holy Spirit" (2 Peter 1:21). The men who wrote the biblical books were not inventing things. Neither were they automatons. They were real people in real historical times with real DNA writing according to their historical settings and their personalities. But the authorship of Scripture was dual. It was, for instance, both Jeremiah and God, because Jeremiah was picked up and carried along. Indeed, in Jeremiah's case, God said, "Behold, I have put my words in your mouth" (1:9). He did so without violating Jeremiah's distinct personality, and he then wrote the very Word of God. This is why we study the Bible—because this is a book that exists as a result of the out-breathing of the Holy Spirit.

Concerning the identity of the Helper, we could go on ad infinitum, but we must be selective rather than exhaustive. His identity is as "another Helper." The word translated as "another" here is *allos*, not *heteros*. Jesus promised a Helper of the same kind rather than of a different kind. The Spirit is the *parakletos*, the one who comes alongside. Jesus said He would "be with you forever ... he dwells with you and will be in you" (John 14:16-17). In other words, His ministry is both permanent and personal. (Begg, 2020, Retrieved from: https://www.ligonier.org/blog/five-truths-about-holy-spirit/)

And, that is all.

And really, *this*, is everything.

# Conclusion

## "I AM"

*"Thy word is a lamp unto my feet, and a light unto my path."*
*(Psalm 119:105)*

... and here it is, another day. Once again, I've broken my fast and am thanking God for getting me through the night; giving me one more day to breathe in His Holy Fire and exhale my life in service to Him.

I pray at this breakfast table in both thanksgiving and anticipation. I have re-built my earthly life on the sturdy bedrock of Your Holy Spirit. I train my soul through Your Spirit to say "no" to the riffraff of the enemy.

Your miracles, I know, are endless, and are here for us simply in the asking for them. Another breath, another heartbeat, another thought, another prayer. My Spirit soars. I break my fast with Your Word, sprinkled with grace. My oatmeal has blueberries swimming in fresh cream. I say hello to my Mom and Dad in heaven. I am confident I'll see them again because of You.

This book is lovingly penned in honor of Your Holy Spirit and Your blessings of daily miracles; it's patched together with paragraphs of praise – each letter forming earthly words to describe Your wonderous works. These are word-songs for the earthly deaf, hummed in their heads, a salve for the worldly-handicapped, and mustard seed of hope for anyone who wants to believe but doesn't know where to begin.

Yes! Your Holy Spirit is with us to help us, to comfort us, to lead us, to guide us, just as Jesus promised before He left this place. Your Holy Spirit always was and always will be, patiently loving us, waiting for us to get to know You.

We find You, and like a child in the throes of a new discovery, we gasp our last earthly breath and move into Your Spirit of love and relief, praising with these words, "There You are! You've been with me the whole time after all!"

YOU ARE and I AM, and You loved me before I was even knitted under my Mother's heart. You knew me before I even was even a "me." You created me in that moment of the Spark of Your Divine Holy Spirit. I love you with everything I am; I know now this is why You said I am created by You in Your image and likeness! You've loved me forever and now I love you right back. You always were and always will be – you are the Holy Spirit of my forever God and you flood me with Yourself.

I am Your Temple. You shine through me with the same light that covered the waters of Your New creation in the beginning of time.

The naysayers marvel, the magicians faint. Nothing is impossible with You. Our enemies buckle, we are fearless in fights. You pave the pathway to holiness with Your Word, your carefully crafted love letters written specifically for me. Prayer and praise to Your magnificence changes everything – you are timeless, and we get to spend eternity with You! Please God! Please, God! Send your Holy Spirit and cover this Creation of Yours! Not by power, not by might, by Your Holy Spirit, LORD!

You give us exactly what we need today, You fill us with thankful hearts. How could we not be over the moon in love with You? You wipe away our tears, You heal our hearts. There is gratitude in that toe-stub; even Your pain has a purpose for us.

You know the maps of our hearts, You flood our minds with Your Holy Light so we can see in our Spirits how faith in You is not about our own earthly feelings. Feelings aren't facts. Your laser-sharp Spirit silences the enemy.

You have shown mercy to me, I know Your miraculous work firsthand. By the Power of Your everlasting Holy Spirit, You use your people to alleviate the suffering of Your children. Your miracles and supernatural works always were happening and are never-ending.

Thank you for the trials You've put me through. Your generosity is endless. Because of these trials, You have given me the spectacular gift of compassion. I know Your mercy. I know wherever You take me, You will not break me; rather, You will hone me, sharpen me, soften me, and prepare me to serve You better.

There will never be enough days to thank You for Your mercy, LORD. My parents prayed me through my foolish self-inflicted disasters when I was a younger woman. You pulled me out of my problems, shook me up, shook me off, and then put me to work for You. And yes, with my faith the size of a mustard seed, even though I believed the enemy's lies and convinced myself I had used up any smidgeon of grace I had left, Your HOLY SPIRIT, nonetheless, saw that speck of belief in my heart and healed me.

HALLELUJAH!

I join with my Pastor Verissa in this prayer: "There will never be enough days to thank You for Your mercy. There will never be enough time to tell everyone what You do for us. There is not an earthly vessel big enough to measure Your unfathomable love for us. After all, if the sky was parchment and the ocean was an inkwell, there would not be enough of either to write all of our thank you notes to You for everything You do for us every day."

*And they went out and preached everywhere,*
*the Lord working with them and confirming the word,*
*through the accompanying signs.*

*Amen*

*(Mark 16:20)*

# *Epilogue*

## How Do We Arrive at That Holy Place?

Vickie W. laid on the brothel's bed staring at the ceiling, clothed in her most glamorous peignoir. Mumbling the only prayer she ever knew, "Now I lay me down to sleep," she prepared to pull the trigger. A bright white light filled the room; she opened her eyes and saw the wounds on His hands and wrists. His finger was blocking her plan to die.

A few decades earlier, Bill W., the co-founder of Alcoholics Anonymous, had fallen into a very deep depression, the blackest that he had ever known. A hopeless drunk, he laid in a psych ward bed reserved for incorrigibles. Desperate, he cried out,

> "If there is a God, will He show Himself?" (https:// www.recoveryspeakers.com/if-there-is-a-god-will-he-show-himself-bill-w-recounts-his-spiritual-experience/)

The room lit up. He told everyone later, it felt as though he stood on the top of a mountain, that a great clean wind blew; he knew he was free.

Fuchsia Pickett knew not all was well with her soul. She went to a revival, sang a beautiful duet, and left empty-hearted. In Pickett's book, *Divine Revelation*, she describes going home where she fell on her knees under a terrible power of conviction, and in a few moments, like a bolt of lightning, an old-fashioned Methodist salvation experience struck, she was born again! She realized God had heard her prayers after all, and of those she had asked to pray for her.

Divine revelation is not a theory or a doctrine, but rather a living reality. Going through the motions of sitting, standing, kneeling in a building on Sunday is not going to yield any long-lasting benefits. The most it will produce is another imaginary feather in the fake angelic wings we hang up on our empty spiritual wall. In doing not much more than showing up for services, our "doing" becomes our "undoing." Akin to only going through the motions of rowing, we miss the boat completely.

So, how exactly does this revelation thing happen? I certainly have come to know, being intelligent isn't enough. Believing in commitment, consecration and holiness is nice, but it isn't enough either, Pickett tells us. I agree.

Surrender.

Surrender. Give up. Give in. Be surprised!

First, we make that decision to become His. We are born again, made new in His love for us. We know for sure He is with us. We belong to Him.

Then, we surrender. Everything. Every single thing from the hairs on our heads, to the thoughts under the hairs on our heads; we surrender our very breath itself. We trust Him, without a smidgeon of trepidation.

This Baptism in the Holy Spirit brings us into an entirely new relationship with God. Pickett describes how the veil was suddenly split open between her soul and her Spirit, completely bypassing anything her brain would tell her. She began to truly understand, through divine revelation, the same Scriptures she had studied and taught faithfully for years. She had been touched by our Creator and healed from a painful spine-twisting condition called advanced scoliosis. Her doctors were amazed. Her new Teacher, the blessed Holy Spirit, "came to set up a classroom" (Pickett, 1997, p. 46) in her spirit, a classroom that would always stay open.

She tells us, *"The Word of God is the basis for all Divine Revelation, and knowledge of the Word increases our capacity for receiving that revelation of Christ"* (Pickett, 1997, p.47).

The plethora of contemporary false gospels spring from situational ethics, a result of relative thinking. True Biblical Christianity is the revelation of God; it is not man-made faith. The Word of God is complete (Rev 22:18-19), not to be added, not a Word removed. Born again and filled with His Holy Spirit, we yield to the Holy Spirit when reading His Holy Word, allowing Him to teach us.

As a hearing-impaired person, I do not take sounds for granted. It wasn't always this way for me. There was a time I had to cultivate quietness. Now, I do not have that choice. I live in a mostly quiet world, there are times I wonder if God dampened my hearing so I could hear Him better. "Be still and know I am God" (Psalms 46:10). So, I sit still, hearing impaired, and ready.

I, like Ms. Pickett, am grateful for the blessed opportunity to learn His Word in a deeper, life-changing way every day. My other senses heightened, I can see the light and dark of this world.

After earning two doctoral degrees, she reports how an intellectual approach to understanding Scripture will not result in a correct interpretation of the truth. She considered how all language is under the curse of sin, making the Holy Spirit's revelation necessary to reveal the correct intent of His Word. "The Holy Spirit wrote the Bible and then moves in our Temples to teach it to us" she says (Pickett, 1997, p. 83). God intends for His Temples - each one of us - to be filled with His glory, His living Word – Christ Himself.

Pickett emphasized the need to fill our minds with the Word of God if we expect to receive Divine Revelation. The formula is simple: Obey and submit to His Word, and revelation will come. It's impossible to accept Christ as Savior until we enter into a living relationship with Him. Jesus is not going to be the Holy Bridegroom to strangers.

Knowing Him and knowing about Him are two distinctly different scenarios. Even Satan knows about Him. Even Satan can – and does – quote Scripture.

I came to realize how Bill W., Vickie W., Fuchsia P., and I all have something wonderful in common. As I type this, I am in awe of the company God has allowed me to keep! We each came to know that the value of theological or secular degrees and/or doctrinal positions is shattered in that moment the Holy Spirit revealed Himself to us as our personal "Healer and Baptizer" (Pickett, 1997, p. 120). Prior to Pickett's healing, she was a sincere theologian, repeating what she had been taught instead of being inspired by His Word. There are no people-parrots in Paradise, no matter how colorful or smart they are.

God will, and does, let us know exactly what He wants us to know – when we approach Him with an open heart with holy hands ready to receive His Truth. "God seeks people to worship Him in Spirit and Truth" (John 4:23).

I completely agree with Pickett's description of that place of ultimate Truth we should aspire to attain: The divine moment when we walk away from temptation, that moment when we establish our determination to worship God alone - it is *then* that we experience a personal transfiguration through Christ.

We finally arrive at that holy place where we know He is everything. We choose Him over our family, friends, relatives, doctrinal positions, ambitions and dreams. We say, "Yes" without reservation, free falling into His arms with the complete trust of a child. We become transfigured by the Power of the Holy Spirit within us (Romans 12:1-2).

In closing the door of her inspired thoughts, Pickett wraps her final words around this:

> The idea that we can think Christ's thoughts is almost incomprehensible. Yet Paul declared of us, "We have the mind of Christ" (1 Cor. 2:16). This is true to the extent that we walk in maturity and in divine revelation of the Christ-life within. (Pickett, 1997, p. 151.)

I'll admit, I did not want Pickett's book to end. I felt sad. I felt like I was walking away from a mentor I'd never met. I wanted to sit down with Fuchsia and gab about flowers, scones and Noah's Ark. I wanted to make her a pot of tea and twine orchids together in a necklace of flowers to frame her face.

Instead, I will share these gems from her book with you while thanking Dr. Bowen, my teacher and professor, for bringing this lovely writer into my life. The Body of Christ is amazing, the light in my world shines brighter today because of both of you.

Born again, we arrive at His Holy Place broken. We suffer. Oh, how we suffer. Healed, He fills us with His Holy Spirit. We fall at His feet and thank Him!

Then, we go out and joyfully preach it. Praising Him!

Forever.

For eternity.

Holy Spirit,

Fill every nation, fill every heart with You.

We wait.

Completely in love with You.

# Prayer

*"Therefore, if anyone is in Christ, the new creation has come:*
*The old has gone, the new is here!"*

*(2 Cor. 5:17)*

It's not enough to know about Jesus. The adversary knows about Him, too. When I made the decision to truly know Jesus everything changed. I came to realize my life was not my own. I had to cast off my old ways of thinking and start doing things differently in an effort to begin reconciling myself to Him. Every person making that decision becomes a new creation, not merely improved or reformed, but truly transformed. Life looks – and is – completely different.

We begin to see His Creation with new eyes; we are given a heart of compassion. We don't just ignore sin, we avoid it. There is a big difference between continuing to sin and continuing to live in sin. It's impossible to reach sinless perfection in this life; however, the redeemed Christian is being sanctified day by day, sinning less and less and truly cringing each time we miss the mark. After all, *we are now freed from sin and it no longer has power over us. (Romans 6:6-7)* We begin to walk in the fruit of the Spirit which is *"love, joy, peace, longsuffering, kindness, goodness, faithfulness, gentleness, self-control." (Galatians 5:22).*

We learn how to walk in the awesome Power of the Most High God.

*Jesus said to them, "Go into all the world and preach the gospel to all creation. Whoever believes and is baptized will be saved, but whoever does not believe will be condemned. And these signs will accompany those who believe: In my name they will drive out demons; they will speak in new tongues; they will pick up snakes with their hands; and when they drink deadly poison, it will not hurt them at all; they will place their hands on sick people, and they will get well." (Mark 16:15-18)*

Study the Bible and ask the Holy Spirit to read it with you. The more we pray, the more His Holy Word begins to work in our lives. We begin to produce in us what God intended for us all along. We become more like Him.

We become aware that our "death" is the end of our old sinful nature which was nailed to the cross with Christ. It was buried with Him, and just as He was raised up by the Father, so are we raised up to *"walk in newness of life" (Romans 6:4)*.

That old me had to die, Lord Jesus. You knew it, I knew it. Thank you for pulling me out of the mess I made of the life you gave me. Thank you for this second chance! Please help me to stay on the right path with You. Amen

(Nelson and Krueger, 2019, p.198)

# Bibliography

Anonymous. (2003). *Spiritual Awakenings: Journeys of the Spirit*. New York, NY: AA Grapevine, Inc.

Biblegateway.com (1995–2017). Zondervan Corp.

Bowen, R. L., Th.D. (2008). *Altar Ministry Handbook: A Guide for Altar Workers*. Xulon Press.

Brand, Dr. Paul, and Yancey, Philip. (1993). *The Gift of Pain*. Grand Rapids, MI: Zondervan.

Buckingham, Jamie. (1999). *Daughter of Destiny: The Authorized Biography of Kathryn Kuhlman*. Newberry, FL: Bridge Logos.

Dvorak, Becky. (2012). *Dare to Believe: The True Power of Faith to Walk in Divine Healing and Miracles*. Shippensburg, PA: Destiny Image Publishers.

Horn, Trent. (2019). *Counterfeit Christs*. El Cajon, CA: Catholic Answers, Inc.

Howard-Browne, Dr. Rodney. (1992). *The Touch of God.* Tampa, FL: Revival Ministries International.

Kendall, R. T. (2003). *The Anointing: Yesterday, Today, Tomorrow.* Lake Mary, FL: Charisma House.

Kendall, R. T. (2013). *These Are the Days of Elijah.* Bloomington, MN: Chosen Books.

Kendall, R. T. (2014). *40 Days with the Holy Spirit.* Lake Mary, FL: Charisma House

Krueger, Kimberly, and Nelson, Luanne. (2018). *A Few Words of Comfort for the Grieving.* FEW International Publications.

Krueger, Kimberly, and Nelson, Luanne. (2017a). *Holy, Whole and Fit.* FEW International Publications.

Krueger, Kimberly, and Nelson, Luanne. (2017b). *The Miracle Effect.* FEW International Publications.

Kuhlman, Kathryn. (2019). *Nothing Is Impossible with God.* Kathryn Kuhlman Foundation. Newberry, FL: Bridge Logos.

# Bibliography

Kuhlman, Kathryn. (1997). *The Greatest Power in the World.* Kathryn Kuhlman Foundation. Newberry, FL: Bridge Logos.

McKenna, Briege. (1987). *Miracles Do Happen: The Inspiring True Story of The World-Famous Healer and The Reality of Miracles.* Dublin, Ireland: Veritas Publications.

Nelson, Luanne. (2019). *Tipping Tables: The Seven Deadly Sins and Stories of Redemption.* Milwaukee, WI: Nico11 Publishing and Design.

Nelson, Luanne. (2016). Interview with my pastor. Naomi Ministries. Non-published.

Nelson, Luanne, and Krueger, Kimberly. (2019). *A Few Words on Your Identity in Christ.* FEW International Publications.

Nelson, Luanne, and Krueger, Kimberly. (2018). *The Breakthrough Effect.* FEW International Publications.

Pickett, Fuschia. (1997). *Receiving Divine Revelation.* Lake Mary, FL: Charisma House.

Praying Medic. (2013). *Divine Healing Made Simple.* Gilbert, AZ: Inkity Press.

Reece, Erik. (2005, December 1). Jesus without the miracles: Thomas Jefferson's Bible and the Gospel of Thomas. *Harper's Magazine,* v. 311, n. 1867. Archived from the original on February 18, 2006.

Roberts, Oral. (1947). *If You Need Healing, Do These Things.* Garden City, NY: Country Life Press.

Sumrall, Lester. (1982). *The Gifts and Ministries of the Holy Spirit.* New Kensington, PA: Whitaker House.

Wigglesworth, Smith. (2006). *On Prayer, Power and Miracles.* Shippensburg, PA: Destiny Image Publishers, Inc.

Wigglesworth, Smith. (1999). *Smith Wigglesworth on Healing.* New Kensington, PA: Whitaker House.

Wood, Gary. (2013). *Miracles: God's Heavenly Touch on Man.* Kingwood, TX: RevMedia Publishing.

Yancey, Philip. (1997). *What's So Amazing About Grace?* Grand Rapids, MI: Zondervan.

# Bibliography

## Online References

Author Unknown, Blog Post. (2019). The Great Physician. Retrieved from

https://www.backtothebible.org/post/the-great-physician-1

Begg, Alistair. (2020). Five Truths About the Holy Spirit. Retrieved from

https://www.ligonier.org/blog/five-truths-about-holy-spirit/

Cheddie, Denver. (2001). The Anointing. Retrieved from https://bibleissues.org/anointing1.html

DeGarmo, Shannon. (2019). What We Need to Remember When God Says No. Retrieved from

https://www.crosswalk.com/faith/

Doctor, Dr. Jonathan. (2019). The Transfer of Anointing. Retrieved from www.fofmc.net

*Hagin, Kenneth E. (2017). Faith v. Feelings.* Retrieved from https://www.hopefaithprayer.com/faith/kenneth-hagin-faith-lesson-no-7-faith-vs-feelings/

Ham, Steve. (2015). What Is the Image of God? Retrieved from https://answersingenesis.org/genesis/what-is-image-of-god/

Houghton, Al. (2020, July). Creative Miracles V. *Word at Work* Newsletter. Retrieved from https://wordatwork.org/wp-content/uploads/2012/06/2012-07.pdf

Leonard, Tasha Cobbs. Official Music Video for "Your Spirit" by Tasha Cobbs Leonard ft. Kierra Sheard taken from the album "Heart. Passion. Pursuit." Music video by Tasha Cobbs Leonard performing "Your Spirit" ft. Kierra Sheard. (C) 2017 Capitol Christian Music Group, Inc. Retrieved from https://www.youtube.com/watch?v=BZT8jqsc8lQ

*NIH Funded Study. (2011).* Zinc 'sparks' fly from egg within minutes of fertilization. Retrieved from https://www.nih.gov/news-events/news-releases/zinc-sparks-fly-egg-within-minutes-fertilization

Praying Medic. (2020). The Great Awakening. Retrieved from: www.prayingmedic.com

(https://www.recoveryspeakers.com/if-there-is-a-god-will-he-show-himself-bill-w-recounts-his-spiritual-experience/)

Schapiro, Jeff. (2013). Humanists Create 'New Jefferson Bible;' Deliver Copies to Obama, Congress. Retrieved from https://www.christianpost.com/news/humanists-create-new-jefferson-bible-deliver-copies-to-obama-congress.html

# Bibliography

Spector, Nicole. (2017). This is Your Brain on Prayer and Meditation. Retrieved from https://www.nbcnews.com/better/health/your-brain-prayer-meditation-ncna812376

Staff at BibleStudyTools. (2020). I Will Never Leave You Nor Forsake You. Retrieved from

https://www.biblestudytools.com/topical-verses/i-will-never-leave-you-nor-forsake-you/

Thomas, Adam. (2017). The Spiritual Desert. Retrieved from https://wherethewind.com/2016/12/12/the-spiritual-desert/

Williams, Greg. (2016). Brain Images Reveal First Physical Evidence that Prayers Reduce Cravings in Alcoholics Anonymous Members. Retrieved from https://nyulangone.org/news/brain-images-reveal-first-physical-evidence-prayers-reduce-cravings-alcoholics-anonymous-members

# About the Author

Luanne Nelson loves sharing stories of her trials and victories through the powerful, healing grace of God. Her recent collaborative book, *Tipping Tables - The Seven Deadly Sins and Stories of Redemption,* includes a collection of stories from writers world-wide, sharing their personal experiences of God's magnificent love and His unfathomable mercy.

She was miraculously healed of a spinal injury, and also was released by the power of God from addictions over twenty years ago. Baptized in the Holy Spirit, she ministers the Word of God as an ordained street preacher through Naomi Ministries.

Luanne studied English Literature at Westminster College in Pennsylvania, and Journalism at Marquette University in Milwaukee, Wisconsin. This book is a copy of Luanne's thesis, written while earning her Master's Degree at Midwest Bible College in Milwaukee, Wisconsin.

Many years ago, Luanne was named one of the most interesting people in the city by *Milwaukee Magazine*; her friends call her "a force of nature." Filled with His Holy Spirit, Luanne Nelson is a joyful witness, a warrior, and a wayfarer for Jesus Christ. Please visit her website at www.LuanneNelson.com

*"And we know that God causes all things to work together*
*for good to those who love God,*
*to those who are called according to His purpose."*
*Romans 8:28*

# About Naomi's Street People

*"Go ye therefore, and teach all nations, baptizing them in the name of the Father, and of the Son, and of the Holy Spirit"* (Matthew 28:19).

*"And He said unto them, 'Go ye into all the world, and preach the gospel to every creature. He that believeth and is baptized shall be saved; but he that believeth not shall be damned. And these signs shall follow them that believe; in my name shall they cast out devils; they shall speak with new tongues they shall take up serpents; and if they drink any deadly thing, it shall not hurt them; they shall lay hands on the sick, and they shall recover. they shall take up serpents; and if they drink any deadly thing, it shall not hurt them; they shall lay hands on the sick, and they shall recover"* (Mark 16:15-18 KJV).

*"And this gospel of the kingdom shall be preached in all the world for a witness unto all nations; and then shall the end come"* (Matthew 24:14 KJV).

*"As you go, proclaim this message: 'The kingdom of heaven has come near.' Heal the sick, raise the dead, cleanse those who have leprosy, drive out demons. Freely you have received; freely give"* (Matthew 10:7-8 NIV).

We are street teachers and preachers for the Glory of Jesus Christ. We are called to be His servants; followers who walk in faith, obeying His Word by preaching the Gospel. We teach. We preach. We baptize. We seek the blessed opportunity to lead people to salvation in the knowledge of Christ Jesus through the Holy Spirit; He gives the increase.

We are spiritual gardeners, continually sowing new seeds, watering and nurturing those seeds with the Word of God. Every day we pray we will have the opportunity to lead people to Jesus. We pray, we practice compassion. God is love, He knows the maps of our hearts. He knows the map of your heart. You are His beautiful creation.

Our ministry does not have a church building, we gather in homes, in restaurants, and on the streets to pray together. Jesus ministered outside, enjoyed dinner with friends at home, served dinner on mountainsides as described in Mark 8:1-9.

We are on the streets where you live—you'll find us in grocery stores, at the hardware store, at the post office—wherever you go! We know the power and the love of God and we want you to know, too!

We have been freely given His mercy, His Grace and we know His Love. Our God, the Creator of Justice and Mercy. Get to know Him. Seriously. Know His Goodness, Mercy, Forgiveness, and Love.

We are thankful to Jesus—He taught us how to truly love, how to serve, He promised us eternal life and delivered on this promise by His terrible death and Holy Resurrection. It's all spelled out specifically in His Holy Word.

His Holy Spirit is at work: He works through each one of us— we are His servants until He returns in Glory! Ask the Holy Spirit to give you eyes to read, ears to hear, and a heart to understand His Word. You'll discover how His Word replaces bitterness with joy, despair with hope, and doubt with faith.

Trust Him.

# Other Books With
# Luanne Nelson

### Tipping Tables -
### The Seven Deadly Sins & Stories of Redemption
A Study in Redemption, a Collection of Beautiful Stories
(Nico 11 Publishing & Design)

### The Miracle Effect
A Collection of Stories
(FEW International Publications)

### The Breakthrough Effect
A Collection of Stories
(FEW International Publications)

### Becoming, Whole, and Fit
Devotional
(FEW International Publications)

### A FEW words of Comfort for the Grieving
Devotional
#1 Amazon Bestseller

### A FEW Words On Your Identity in Christ
Devotional

To order these books, or for more information,
visit Luanne's website:
www.LuanneNelson.com

# A Special Thanks

## Special Thanks to Midwest Bible College

*"Arise, shine; for your light has come,*
*And the glory of the LORD has risen upon you.*
*For behold, darkness will cover the earth*
*And deep darkness the peoples;*
*But the LORD will rise upon you*
*And His glory will appear upon you."*

*Isaiah 60:1-2*

The college is fully accredited through the Association of Independent Christian Colleges and Seminaries.

Midwest Bible College
P.O. Box 270184
Milwaukee, Wisconsin 53227
Phone: (414) 546-1248
Email: info@midwestbiblecollege.org

Website: MidwestBibleCollege.org

CPSIA information can be obtained
at www.ICGtesting.com
Printed in the USA
BVHW031410180521
607630BV00005B/418